WES ANDERSON

THE ICONIC FILMMAKER AND HIS WORK

IAN NATHAN

Brimming with creative inspiration, how-to projects and useful information to enrich your everyday life, Quarto Knows is a favourite destination for those pursuing their interests and passions. Visit our site and dig deeper with our books into your area of interest: Quarto Creates, Quarto Cooks, Quarto Homes, Quarto Lives, Quarto Drives, Quarto Explores, Quarto Gifts, or Quarto Kids.

First published in 2020 by White Lion Publishing,
an imprint of The Quarto Group.
The Old Brewery, 6 Blundell Street
London, N7 9BH,
United Kingdom
T (0)20 7700 6700
www.QuartoKnows.com

A catalogue record for this book is available from the British Library.

ISBN 978 0 71125 599 9
Ebook ISBN 978 0 71125 600 2

10 9 8 7 6 5

Designed by Sue Pressley and Paul Turner, Stonecastle Graphics Ltd

Printed in China

WES ANDERSON

THE ICONIC FILMMAKER AND HIS WORK

IAN NATHAN

UNOFFICIAL AND UNAUTHORISED

WHITE
LION
PUBLISHING

CONTENTS

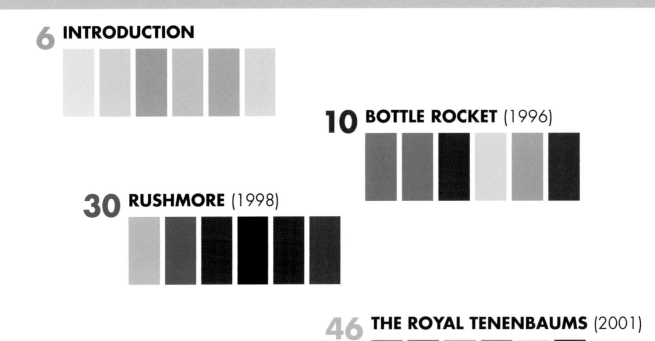

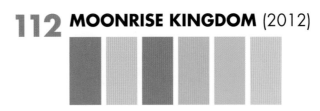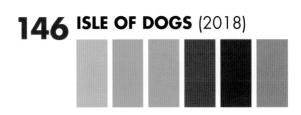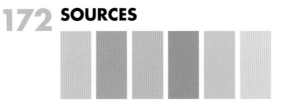

INTRODUCTION

'The secret, I don't know ... I guess you've just gotta find something you love to do and then ... do it for the rest of your life.'[1]

Max Fischer, *Rushmore*

In the very first scene of Wes Anderson's very first film, *Bottle Rocket*, the self-involved hero Anthony (Luke Wilson) escapes from a mental hospital by knotting his bed sheets together and lowering himself to the ground below. This elaborate escape plan has been hatched by his best pal, Owen Wilson's incurable schemer Dignan, currently hiding in the bushes. What Dignan doesn't realize is that Anthony's time at the institute was entirely voluntary. He was free to leave at any point – out the front door. 'He just got so excited about the thing,' Anthony tells his bemused doctor, 'I didn't have the heart to tell him.'[2]

You could say that the Texan-born filmmaker's fleet of ten brilliant, perplexing, idiosyncratic and pristine films, from *Bottle Rocket* to *The French Dispatch*, has stuck rigidly to Dignan's way of thinking. Never go out the front door when you can shinny to terra firma using a makeshift rope, like they might in a great adventure story in a book or a film. Reality needs enhancing.

We should also take note that Anderson's menagerie of complicated protagonists begins with a character wrestling with some unresolved form of unhappiness dubbed 'exhaustion.' It proves a common ailment.

'I guess when I think about it,' mused Anderson, a man who generally does his

Above: Wes Anderson's debut film *Bottle Rocket*, featuring his real-life housemates and friends, brothers Luke and Owen Wilson. It worked as a kind of comic exaggeration of events in his own life.

Opposite: Anderson at the Rome Film Festival in 2015. He cultivates a distinctive sense of personal style to match his tailored films.

musing in film form, 'one of the things I like to dramatize, and what is sometimes funny, is someone coming unglued.'[3]

My first Wes was *Rushmore*. What I loved so much about this oddball love triangle was that I couldn't quite pin down why I loved it so much – it was hilarious but never felt wholly like a comedy; heartfelt and sad, but also cynical and knowing. It was full of outrageous, teeth-itchingly embarrassing behaviour, yet somehow comforting. And so beautifully *arranged* – I can think of no better word. From there (with a particular leaning toward the brotherly entanglements of *The Darjeeling Limited*, though every time

I check into *The Grand Budapest Hotel* I still find it magnificent), I willingly threw myself down the rabbit hole and into the bi-polar Brigadoon of Andersonland.

Ask Anderson why he assembles his tales of hapless souls with the precision of a Swiss watch, and he would greet the enquiry with bafflement. How else would he make them? 'I have a way of filming things and staging them and designing sets,' he once said. 'There were times when I thought I should change my approach, but in fact this is what I like to do. It's sort of like my handwriting as a movie director. And somewhere along the way, I think I've made the decision: I'm going to write in my own handwriting.'[4]

He really can't help being Wes Anderson. His films are extensions of his life and personality, right down to the corduroy suits, alphabetized bookshelves, arty film references, and Bill Murray in badger form. There are times they are almost about themselves – think about the literal film crew of *The Life Aquatic with Steve Zissou* or M. Gustave's determined attempts to maintain civility in the face of chaos in *The Grand Budapest Hotel*. Tormented artists are to be found throughout.

He could never make a sequel; it would be undignified. Yet however diverse the setting (from downtown Dallas to Northern India to dystopian Japan) and subject (from oceanography to fascism to dogs), his films feel intimately connected, a self-contained universe. He has become an institution.

The truth is, Anderson is getting more Andersonian with age. *The French Dispatch* is a ferment of storytelling with a dizzying cast of willing A-listers.

All of which is why he is such a beguiling subject for a book (and he is a professed lover of film books). There are few directors in such control of their process, where scripts go hand in hand

with directorial stratagems and mood boards revealing colour schemes, fabric choices, and set-square-precise camera moves. What a character wears and how they adorn their specific milieu helps define who they are. Art direction and costume design are inseparable from plot-twist and backstory. Recall how each of the crew's scarlet beanies in *The Life Aquatic with Steve Zissou* are worn at a slightly differently angle. You know Anderson oversaw each and every hat placement. He makes films on a molecular level. They are their own ecosystem, an ocean where dark currents flow beneath the dappled surface.

'There is something about all this obvious fakery that draws us closer and makes us gasp for breath,'[5] noted writer Chris Heath, pondering the collected works in *GQ*. The mixture of 'fact and fiction and feeling'[6] has the familiarity of a half-remembered dream. His movies may not strictly speaking be set in reality, but they are always about real things.

On set Anderson is convivial, charming, and unsparing in his drive for perfection. 'Wes is kind of an incredibly kind, patient slave driver,'[7] joked Bob Balaban, who, commencing with *Moonrise Kingdom*, has become one of a growing troupe of devoted actors, led by muse-in-chief Murray. Balaban was also hitting on a truth. Anderson has made it a lifelong policy 'not to do something that eventually I am going to hate.'[8] He may be slender as a crane, and not known to raise his voice, but never doubt who is in charge. Even Gene Hackman had to learn that.

What Wes-averse critics deride as indulgence, a collection of sweet, kitschy, suffocating bagatelles that make less of a canon than a patisserie window, I would classify as one of the most consistent and endlessly fascinating filmographies of modern times (albeit in suave, nostalgic ways). What makes Anderson's films so exquisitely familiar

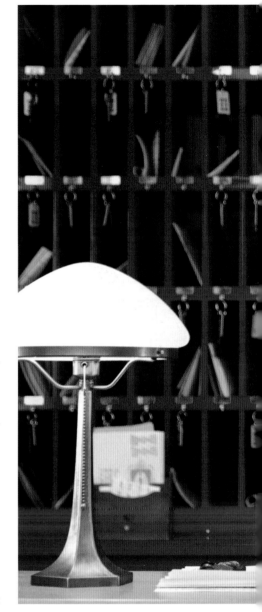

is that they are so different from what anyone else is doing.

As Peter Bogdanovich, director and critic, with a catalogue of esteemed film books to his name, described the work of his good friend: 'With a Wes Anderson film, you know who the devil made it, yet his style is as difficult to describe as only the best styles are, because they're subtle.'[9]

Across the forthcoming pages, lit
up with beautiful photographs, I will
examine each film in neat, chronological
order (naturally), discuss its origins
and inspirations, something of its
making, and make my own attempt
to fathom the Andersonian mystery.
What M. Gustave would deem 'faint
glimmers of civilization ...'[10]

Above: The great concierge
M. Gustave H. (Ralph Fiennes)
presides over the front desk of
The Grand Budapest Hotel.
He can be read as an avatar
for the director: a man of
refinement and taste, good in
a tight spot.

BOTTLE ROCKET

For his first film, Wes Anderson turned life into art. This cult tale of three Dallas friends attempting to get into crime was born out of the young writer-director's early experiences and a slice of luck

This being a survey of the life and career of Wes Anderson, we should begin with a story within a story within a story. Like one of those nesting Matryoshka dolls to which his movies are so often compared. The ones you keep opening until you get to the real doll at the centre in perfect miniature.

So, let's begin on the day the young Anderson returned home to find a pamphlet on top of the refrigerator entitled 'Coping with the Very Troubled Child'.[1] He knew at once it concerned him and not his two brothers: 'They were never going to make a mistake and think it was themselves.'[2] They were adjusting to their parents' divorce far better than he was. Or for that matter, twelve-year-old Suzy Bishop in *Moonrise Kingdom*, who finds the same pamphlet on top of the family icebox and reacts to her mother's affair by running off with her not-quite lover and singularly unpopular boy scout Sam Shakusky – also considered by his foster folks to be emotionally disturbed.

A sensitive, shall we say complex boy, Anderson has mentioned many times in interview that his parents' split was the most 'traumatic'[3] event of his childhood, something he's been working out in his charmingly quirky yet deeply melancholic collection of

movies. *The Royal Tenenbaums* revolves around the emotional wreckage of a trio of grown-up child prodigies abandoned by their no-good father.

Where were we? Oh yes, the next story. Whether inspired by his mother resorting to extra-parental advice or not, it was around this time Anderson proposed to both his parents that he be allowed to move to Paris, alone, at the tender age of twelve. He provided his own handouts to better explain the advantages. 'I had written out all these reasons,' he explained: 'the science programme in French schools was stronger, and so on.'[4] Though neatly packaged, they'd been entirely fabricated from what classmates had told him, and 'had absolutely no basis in reality,'[5] he confirmed. He simply imagined that life would be so much better in the French capital – historic home to such expatriate luminaries and Anderson favourites as F. Scott Fitzgerald and Ernest Hemingway.

His parents sensibly informed him this was not even remotely on the cards, but today Anderson, an American filmmaker whose work is infused with the aroma of Europe, spends half the year, if not more, in his apartment overlooking the artistic quarter of Montparnasse.

Above: Wes Anderson at a tender 26, still more the Houston-born skater kid than the dapper, worldly filmmaker to come.

Opposite: The release poster for Anderson's neglected debut, much of its subject matter drawn from the years he and stars Luke and Owen Wright spent cohabiting in Dallas.

They're not really criminals,
but everybody's got to have a dream.

BOTTLE ROCKET

Which brings us to the next story. When the junior Anderson began acting up at his plush Houston prep, his savvy (and frankly pivotal) fourth-grade teacher found the only way to corral his wandering mind was to allow him to put on his own plays, just as deeply troubled and slyly gifted tenth-grader Max Fischer directs extravagant productions in *Rushmore*.

It was a points system. For each week Anderson did *not* get into trouble, the teacher would award him points. When he gained enough of them, she let him put on one of his five-minute plays in the school. 'And I feel like in a way what I do now is vaguely, you know, continuing from then,'[6] he said.

Anderson revealed his ambition both in subject matter and form from the very start. His take on a crucial part of local history, the Battle of the Alamo, amounted, he said, to 'one big war scene.'[7] He played Davy Crockett. Like Max in *Rushmore*, he always reserved the best parts for himself. His plays, he recalled, were 'usually big crowd pleasers,'[8] heavily influenced by film and television shows: they included versions of *King Kong* and a 'loose adaptation'[9] of *The Headless Horseman* where the decapitated protagonist was the hero. Another production, *The Five Maseratis*, took place, as the title suggests, with the cast sat in a quintet of Maseratis. Later, from the vantage point of experience, he admitted the show was 'kind of static.'[10]

Anderson, you will not be shocked to learn, was a precocious, gifted child, perhaps even a prodigy. He still is. There is an argument he remains that troubled twelve-year-old boy, now given the perfect outlet for his and all of our sorrows.

Above: Wannabe criminal wannabes – brothers Luke and Owen Wilson, local coffee shop manager turned actor Kumar Pallana and Bob Musgrave, with director and flatmate Anderson.

Opposite: As the script developed *Bottle Rocket* became less of a comedy heist movie and far more the study of devoted but often unhealthy friendship.

If you wanted to sum up the world according to Wes, then it is the portrayal of very messed-up people in very orderly films. Everything feels fake but the feelings. Given that each of these films, to differing degrees, peers back into the circumstances of Anderson's life, biographical detail is never far away. He invests so much of who he is into the fabric of his storytelling: memories, locations, names, the casting of actual friends, acquaintances and neighbourhood coffee-shop proprietors, and his bespoke sense of style. Anderson could never take on another's script to direct. He can only serve his personal whims. Which is why we call him an *auteur*.

So we must begin with the backstory, a montage dressed in the detail of the early years of Wesley Wales Anderson, born in Houston, Texas, on 1 May 1969. Listen carefully, all of this will prove relevant.

Anderson is the middle of three brothers. Mel came first, Eric Chase afterwards. Mel has grown up to be a doctor; Eric Chase an artist. Many of his younger sibling's paintings adorn Anderson's movies and DVD covers. Real brothers, or close friends played by real brothers, feature in *Bottle Rocket*, *The Royal Tenenbaums* and *The Darjeeling Limited*. There are plenty of brotherhoods too, be they oceanographers, Khaki Scouts, or a secret society of concierges from Europe's finest pre-war hotels.

His mother, Texas Ann Anderson (née Burroughs) was a onetime archaeologist, and the boys spent time on digs unearthing relics. But as needs must, raising the boys alone, she became a real estate agent. Note that Anjelica Huston's Etheline, wounded matriarch of the wounded Tenenbaum brood, is an archaeologist by trade. Texas also came from fitting literary stock. Her

grandfather was Edgar Rice Burroughs, creator of *Tarzan*, and some of his DNA has made its way down to Anderson, who describes his films as adventures. Anderson's father, Melver Leonard Anderson, worked in advertising and publicity, and supplies ancestry from Sweden, land of miserablist master Ingmar Bergman.

The knots of family, bound by blood, friendship, dysfunction or deep-sea exploration, form the cornerstone of Anderson's preoccupations.

Compared to the standard Texan image of the high school jock/grouchy loner, Anderson's worldly viewpoint, dapper dress and intellectual pursuits imply a New Yorker exiled on an alien planet. He described growing up in Houston as 'hot, humid and full of mosquitoes.'[11] All the same, when he came to use urban Texas as the backdrop to his first two films, he wrapped the Lone Star State in

dreamlike warmth. When asked, he identifies as Texan, and his voice, never raised, possesses a soft Southern accent.

His parents were wealthy enough to send him to St. John's, a prestigious prep school in Houston (for more details see *Rushmore*). Nevertheless, he went through a phase where he 'became obsessed with being rich.'[12] His first major project was assembling a 'book of mansions'[13] filled with drawings of upscale estates, and detailing every luxury, with Rolls Royces in the driveway like the Bentley Herman Blume drives in *Rushmore*.

There followed a phase where he drew people living in trees; whole communities with homes in the branches. The upwardly mobile Fox family take (short-lived) residence inside an upscale tree in *Fantastic Mr. Fox*. A treehouse figures in *Moonrise Kingdom* too, while in *The Royal Tenenbaums*, among morose Margot's early plays is one called *The Levinsons in the Trees*. Anderson was deeply taken with Johann David Wyss's *The Swiss Family Robinson* and its 1971 Disney adaptation, featuring the construction of an elaborate treehouse.

He and his brother Mel actually cut a hole in their roof so they could enter the house from a different angle. They planned it all out. It took days. Anderson remembered his father's fury. He had never seen him like that.

There were so many plans, charts and blueprints. Sat at a tilted draftsman's table his father bought for him in more agreeable times, Anderson spent hours drawing complex pictures, refitting the world into a neater, sweeter shape. He was intent first on becoming an architect and later a writer. 'I guess part of what I do with these movies,' he said, 'is a bit of a combination of those things.'[14]

The first film he can remember seeing is *The Pink Panther*, at a revival house in downtown Houston. He saw the Disney cartoons there too. The first time he ever considered the presence of a filmmaker was after perusing the family's box set of Alfred Hitchcock movies. He was amazed to see the director's name so prominently displayed on it, above any of the actors. He was equally amazed at the contents of the box, especially *Rear Window*, with its readymade tenement block.

He was not immune from a geek phase, with a distinct memory of flicking through a book of *Star Wars* concept art by Ralph McQuarrie in his doctor's waiting room. And there was Steven Spielberg; he loved Spielberg. Especially the *Indiana Jones* films with their arch, adventure-book format.

Deciding that filmmaking was his destiny, Anderson took his father's Yashica Super 8 video camera on permanent loan and began making films, usually no more than three minutes long, with carefully devised (cardboard) boxy sets. This is a path trod by many a prospective giant: Spielberg, Peter Jackson, the Coens, and J.J. Abrams. Only with Anderson, even as his budgets and horizons expanded, an essence of the homemade remained.

The Skateboard Four, made in 1976, was the story of quartet of teens who form a skateboard club; it was based, unofficially, on a book by Eve Bunting and Phil Kantz borrowed from the library. Herein gang leader Morgan (played by Anderson) becomes increasingly uptight when a new boy wants to join, shattering the group harmony. Brotherly rivalry and the fraught nature of leadership have evolved into key motifs. Plus, that sounds a lot like the plot of *The Life Aquatic with Steve Zissou*.

Anderson would convince his brothers to perform. Eric Chase would end up providing many of the rather impressionistic 'making-of' extras for Anderson DVDs and performed the

voice of the hip fox Kristofferson in *Fantastic Mr. Fox* and Secretary McIntire of the Khaki Scouts in *Moonrise Kingdom*.

Further early Andersons, including micro-versions of *Indiana Jones*, were lost to posterity when the camera and

reels were stolen from the family car.
Anderson trawled the pawnshops of
Houston to no avail. He has let them go.
Maybe it was for the best, he reflected:
'you couldn't say they showed a lot of
promise.'[15]

Above: Musgrave and
brothers Owen and Luke
Wilson (not, as it happens,
playing brothers) on location
at one of Anderson's many
old haunts in Dallas.

Bottle Rocket   15

Aged 18, Anderson headed to the University of Texas in Austin to major in philosophy, which figures. He was once again set on being a writer, maybe of journalism, novels or plays. He took a course in playwriting, which took place around a big table in Benedict Hall. There were nine participants, and Anderson and this blond character would sit, unmoved, at opposite corners. Neither spoke a word.

The guy was named Owen Wilson, and he and Anderson eventually discovered they had much in common. Both had attended prep school and bore an air of ironic disdain, but were mostly shy. Both were misfits by design. Wilson recalled Anderson as having worn a monocle, which Anderson counter-claimed as entirely untrue. Just some actorly colour used to spice up an anecdote.

The story of the momentous occasion on which they finally spoke to one another takes many shapes. Anderson has it that Wilson sidled up to him in the corridor 'as if they were already close friends,'[16] and asked which classes he should opt for in English. Wilson remembers Anderson singling him out in the same corridor to cast him in his latest play, as he was perfect for one of the parts. *A Night in Tunisia* was a reworking of Sam Shepard's tale of sibling rivalry *True West*. The memory is replayed in *Rushmore* when erstwhile playwright Max Fischer approaches school bully Magnus to take a lead role in his Vietnam play.

Handsome in an off-centred way with that famously wonky nose (broken twice as a teenager), Owen Cunningham Wilson was born in Dallas on 18 November 1968, the middle of three brothers. Andrew, plain handsome, came first and Luke, handsome in a downcast way,

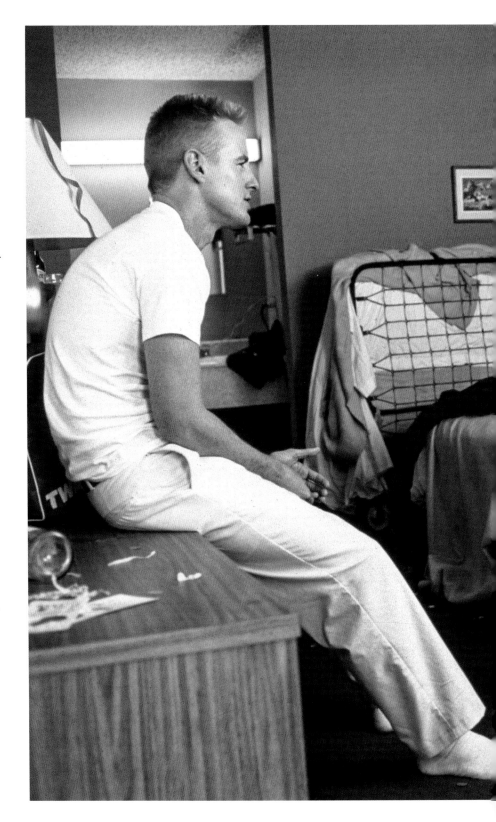

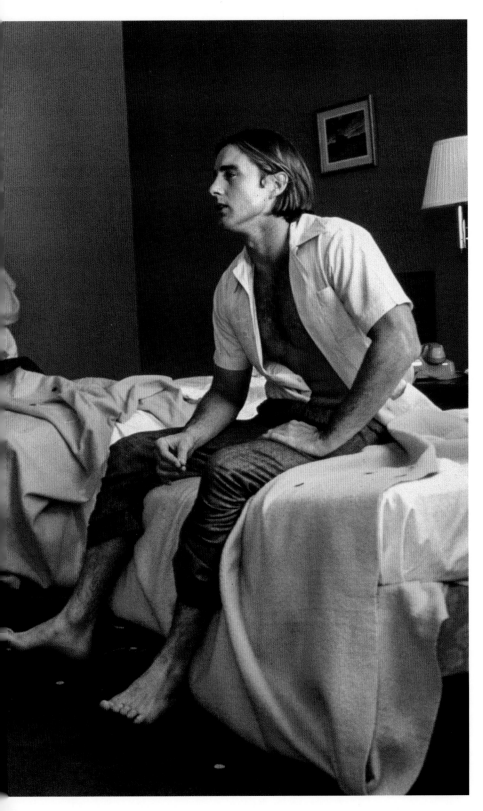

followed. All three are prominent in Anderson's early work. Before university, the fast-talking, troublemaking Wilson had been packed off to military school. He would eventually become one of leading comedy stars of the 2000s.

In the meantime, he and Anderson were to become roommates, writing partners, and fellow travellers on a relatively short and winding road to Hollywood. They found they shared a sense of humour. Or as Anderson said, as if the two things were intimately connected, there was a feeling that 'we might think the same things are sad.'[17]

First though, in order to get the better room (the one with a balcony and bathroom), Anderson struck a deal with Wilson to write his friend's overdue paper on Edgar Allan Poe's short story *The Cask of Amontillado*. Wilson and his ghostwriter got an A+. When the tutor commended the essay as 'magnificent and droll' it became a mutual catchphrase. 'Magnificent and droll'[18] is as good a description as any for Anderson's style.

Movie-obsessed, they would talk into the night about Cassavetes, Peckinpah, Scorsese, Coppola, Malick, Huston and the rise of the Coen brothers. The kind of directors it was cooler to refer to by their last name alone. Anderson always seems to be referred to in full as 'Wes Anderson', as if he's still at school.

Left: Best friends Dignan and Anthony hole up a scruffy local motel after a heist on a bookstore. The Windmill Inn later became a place of pilgrimage for Anderson fanatics.

Thanks to the University's library of films, his tastes matured. The set-up there was curious: students had to sit in a little booth to watch their chosen title. The tapes were not allowed to leave the building. 'You could walk by the other booths and look in a window at each person watching their VHS tape,' he said, recalling a row of screens filled with the European godheads: Truffaut, Godard, Antonioni, Bergman and Fellini. 'Very sort of sixties ... and sort of out of time.'[19]

More than the films, the library had shelves devoted to books on film. Reading is a big deal in Anderson's world. He is a self-confessed bibliophile who collects first editions. His films are filled with books. Some, like *The Royal Tenenbaums* and *The Grand Budapest Hotel*, are confined within the covers of fictional fiction and fictional fact. Authors as tortured

as J.D. Salinger and Stefan Zweig have cast a long shadow over Anderson's collected works, and he wrote a screenplay while sitting in the same chair as his childhood hero Roald Dahl.

For now, he read books on film directors. He read books about the relationship between old movies made by John Ford or Raoul Walsh and the French New Wave. He read collections of director and historian Peter Bogdanovich's articles (they later became pals). He read books on how Spike Lee and Steven Soderbergh got their first films off the ground. And he caught up on the reviews of Pauline Kael, the esteemed critic of the *New Yorker*, fabled for her fizzing erudition and stinging putdowns, whom Anderson had been avidly reading since tenth grade.

All of which accounted for the fact he was once again determined to be a filmmaker.

Above left: Wilson and Anderson on the promotional trail for *Bottle Rocket*. They had met at college, two oddball outsiders sharing an obsession with movies.

Above: Wilson as Dignan getting into character at the shooting range. The target practice sequence, along with much of the start of *Bottle Rocket*, directly repeats scenes from Anderson's original short film.

On graduation in 1991, Anderson and Wilson moved to Dallas and a period of squalor. Dallas was where Wilson's older brother, Andrew, had a job with his father's firm making industrial films, which was as close to the film business as anyone they knew. Bob Wilson, father to the three Wilson boys, was chief executive of the local television station KERA-TV, which had introduced *Monty Python* to North Texas.

Andrew and Owen Wilson, plus from time to time Luke Wilson and pal Bob Musgrave (who would play Bob the diffident getaway driver in the film to come), shared a rundown apartment with Anderson on the insalubrious Thockmorton Street. This was Anderson's first filmmaking family, but no one looks back on those days fondly.

Hygiene was an issue, and, thanks to broken latches, the windows gave little resistance to bitter Texan winters. They berated their landlord to deal with

the problem, but he took no notice. This inspired the following madcap scheme (it is worth noting that nearly all of Anderson's films are propelled by the madcap schemes of verbose dreamers).

Anderson and Wilson staged a self-heist, breaking into their own apartment via an unsecured window and making off with their own stuff, before reporting the crime to the local police. Their landlord was not to be fooled, claiming it looked like an 'inside job'[20] (which it was), and he remained implacable when it came to mending the windows. A draft of a different kind was the welcome result, as Anderson and Wilson used their brief and ineffectual foray into crime as the backbone of a script they called *Bottle Rocket* after the slang term for cheap fireworks that flare briefly into spectacular life.

'The movie emerged from a certain lifestyle we were living at the time,'

Above: Even in his first film, Anderson's penchant for colour coding emerges. Here (in a take on Michael Mann's crime epic *Heat*), yellow boiler suits are set off against the cherry red car.

Opposite: The three leads pose for the camera; the idea of fireworks, echoed in the title, would become a metaphor for the attempts of three lost souls to ignite their lives.

said Anderson. 'Our existence was a little bit unstructured.'[21]

The initial intention was that *Bottle Rocket* would be a gritty crime story under the influence of Anderson and Wilson's beloved Scorsese. But their writing process amounted to roaming around town, thinking up cool scenes. What emerged was the story of three listless friends (to be played by Owen and Luke Wilson and Musgrave) who plan to rob a bookstore – more for kicks than real gain. Raising an initial $2,000 and with more equipment purloined from Andrew, they took to the streets of Dallas to shoot the first scenes of what Anderson saw as 'the opening instalment of the feature.'[22]

He had been experimenting with a series of shorts for a local cable-access channel (a form of community television) where he learned about 'editing and everything'[23] using equipment borrowed from Andrew.

These included a documentary about their landlord, who didn't care for it.

Having produced eight minutes of footage – scenes of a trial raid on a family home based upon their own recent dabbling in self-robbery – they ran out of money.

Wilson then turned to a friend of the family. His father knew L.M. 'Kit' Carson from their public television days in seventies Dallas. Carson was a significant figure in the local film industry, who had starred in Jim McBride's autobiographical docudrama *David Holzman's Diary* and written the acclaimed screenplay for *Paris, Texas*. He knew people in Hollywood.

Quite apart from mentoring Anderson and his gang in the basics of the craft, Carson's immediate advice was to raise more capital from their loved ones, which they duly did. This led to another five minutes, some nips and tucks of the pre-existing material,

and a markedly good thirteen-minute short film.

This early sliver of Anderson's nascent talent bares only slender relation to the scrupulously composed filmmaking we know and love. The rough-and-tumble, handheld black-and-white photography is brazenly lifted from the French New Wave, particularly François Truffaut's streetwise debut *The 400 Blows*. But in the chattering trio we find an early echo of the squabbling brothers of *The Darjeeling Limited*. More immediately, a template was laid down for the debut feature film to come.

It was Carson again who knew what to do next. He had contacts at the Sundance Film Festival (Anderson believed he was on speaking terms with grandee Robert Redford), forge of the American indie scene. Their short was accepted, along with the chance to attend the writing lab – which, Anderson huffed, was a few tiers down from the director's lab.

Here the script came to terms with its true identity. 'It ended up a lot more to do with the friendships of these characters,'[24] said Anderson. Each of the leads – Anthony (Luke Wilson), the chatterbox Dignan (Owen Wilson), and Bob (Musgrave) – is struggling to engage with life. To promote the film, Anderson and Wilson took meetings with the usual indie suspects, including Miramax who were busy fermenting the career of Quentin Tarantino. Miraculously, though, they would end up skipping the indie stage entirely. With a first draft of a potential feature film version of *Bottle Rocket* complete, Carson sent a VHS of the short directly to Hollywood.

Imagine another montage, centred on a tape of the short film being passed from hand to hand up the Hollywood food chain. First Carson gives it to his producer friend Barbara Boyle (*Eight Men Out*), who sends it on to her producer friend Polly Platt. A canny talent spotter who had helped stir Bogdanovich's career into life by producing *The Last Picture Show* (another charming Texan debut and Anderson favourite), Platt could see the raw talent. 'It was unique, unhomogenized, brilliant,'[25] she enthused, before passing it onto James L. Brooks, the director of *Broadcast News* and co-creator of *The Simpsons*, who had a deal with Sony, the power to genuinely get films made, and a taste for unconventional comedy.

Brooks was equally impressed. 'The possession of a real voice is always a marvel, an almost religious thing,'[26] he announced, certain Anderson offered something different from the billions of other ants on the hill. He flew down to Dallas to read the full script, sending shivers through Wilson when he turned on the TV to watch the basketball halfway through. Appalled at the level of subsistence in what he called their

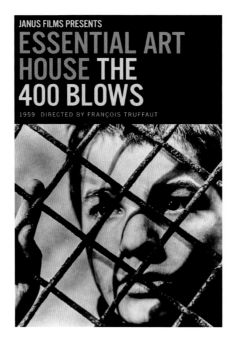

JANUS FILMS PRESENTS

ESSENTIAL ART HOUSE **THE 400 BLOWS**

1959 DIRECTED BY FRANÇOIS TRUFFAUT

Left: The influence of François Truffaut on Anderson's career is huge. *Bottle Rocket's* loose, impulsive style borrows liberally from the French master's freewheeling debut *The 400 Blows.*

'flophouse,'[27] Brooks proposed Anderson and Wilson follow him back to Los Angeles and refine their script into a workable feature film.

So the pair found themselves cohabiting in the comparative luxury of Los Angeles with a sweet *per diem* and an office on the Sony lot in Culver City. There are photos of the boys larking about in golf carts, their eyes filled with the surreal gleam of having made it to the magic kingdom, but it would take two years to get the script right to Hollywood eyes. There was a suspicion they were procrastinating – Brooks would grow frustrated at meetings when they didn't take notes or even have notebooks – but under sufficient supervision from the producer, Sony were persuaded to offer $5 million to expand their short into a studio feature.

Over two months in late 1994, Anderson and his enlarged team (he prefers 'gang'[28]) were back filming among those same Dallas locations, but the jazzy nonchalance of the French New Wave has given way to the first stirrings of the Anderson colourful palette.

The story expands from heist to ludicrous heist in cinema's most leisurely crime spree: first the Luke Wilson character Anthony's home, then the book store (a fine comic sequence), then a safecracking mission on a cold storage facility, joined together with a lot of bickering, soul-searching, and a brief interlude in which Anthony falls in love.

The Windmill Inn Motel, a two-storey oblong of roadside accommodation, could have been purpose-built by Anderson. Here, in Hillsboro (an hour outside the city) where the production was housed and fictionally the heroes lie low, Anthony will fall for Paraguayan maid Inez (the sweet Lumi Cavazos from *Like Water For Chocolate*) – their relationship hilariously mediated via an interpreter as she doesn't possess a word of English. This is first true sighting of the director's sense of whimsy. Here too Anthony will inaugurate the plunge into the insulating embrace of water motif, on permanent loan from *The Graduate*. Since the blossoming of Anderson's career the motel has become the venue

Left: Musgrave, with the Wilson brothers, plays the nominal driver and least enthusiastic member of the gang Bob Mapplethorpe, named in classic Anderson fashion after the famed American photographer.

Below: Anderson and Wilson japing around on go-karts in the lead-up to the film's ill-fated release. Note that a version of go-karting would be one of the extracurricular clubs in *Rushmore*.

of a yearly *Bottle Rocket*-themed fan get-together called the Lovely Soiree.

With Brooks' determination to keep it fresh, the Wilson brothers and Musgrave were retained as leads and the performances are appealingly offbeat and edged in uncertainty. Owen Wilson, who had never set out to act, is the standout as Dignan – still verbalizing every twitching thought, the bright spark with a crew-cut of military spikes. He is the first onscreen avatar for Anderson: an inveterate, often harebrained schemer, a man of inventories and itineraries (we get a glimpse of his seventy-five-year plan for health and happiness written in orange and blue felt-tip) determined to refit reality. Or, as many have surmised, taking the films as a roadmap of the director's inner being, attempting to bring order to chaos.

The production moved with speed from Hickley Cold Storage to the John Gillin Residence (classy homestead to Bob and his bullyboy brother, the explicably nicknamed Future Man played by a wonderfully objectionable Andrew Wilson) designed along pleasing Andersonian lines by Frank Lloyd Wright, and on to St. Mark's School, the prep from which Wilson had been ejected years before, infusing *Bottle Rocket* with the rhythms and sites of shared experience.

The memorably grouchy and not-overly skilled Indian safecracker Kumar is played by Kumar Pallana – who, prior to taking up significant parts in four of Anderson's films, was a sometime vaudevillian and proprietor of the Cosmic Cup, a coffee shop three blocks down from where the director lived.

'No one at that time had any idea that he would become what he has become,'[29] said cinematographer Robert Yeoman, who had received a polite letter from Anderson telling him how much he liked his work on Gus Van Sant's *Drugstore Cowboy* and asking if he might like to join his debut venture (to this day the cameraman has no idea how he got his address). Yeoman has now served as cinematographer on all Anderson's live-action films, witnessing that idiosyncratic rubric evolve: the ninety-degree whip pans, the graceful dolly shots, and two techniques inspired by Martin Scorsese; God's-eye view inserts of notepads and table-tops, and slow-motion montages to classic rock'n'roll (in this case, *2000 Man* by The Rolling Stones).

With the escalating storyline comes the arrival of eccentric local crime lord Mr. Henry, who enrols the boys, chiefly the ever-enterprising Dignan, in his own deceptions. Anderson was keen to cast a big name, and it turned out that he shared an agent with James Caan, Hollywood heavyweight of the seventies, who was available to make an extended cameo (the offer was three days of his

time). There was a tentative approach to Bill Murray, waiting in the wings to take his place as Anderson's North Star.

First Anderson would have to negotiate the wiles of Caan, who arrived late one night accompanied by his karate teacher Tak Kubota, who was duly cast as Rowboat, Mr. Henry's martial arts instructor. Anderson had been awoken by the sound of knocking on his hotel door. Grabbing a robe, he peered out to find the imposing star on his doorstep. 'He was really amped up,'[30] he recalled. Caan wanted to talk about a forthcoming scene and put it to Anderson that they should incorporate some karate elements. 'Let me show ya, let me show ya,'[31] he demanded, and put a defenceless Anderson into a headlock, pulling him into the bathroom to show him how the shot would look in the mirror.

'What is happening here?' wondered Anderson, oxygen hard to come by. 'I am getting my arse kicked by Sonny and

I am in a robe.'[32] The presence of Caan would be the first and bluntest in a series of references to *The Godfather* implanted in his films.

For his part, the actor was bemused but unfazed by Anderson's gnomic approach to storytelling. He did what he always did under such circumstances – went for broke. What you get, broadly speaking, is Caan hamming it up while sporting a topknot like the Samurai from the Akira Kurosawa movies ... though it was only when he found Kubota, his revered mentor, ready to go toe-to-toe in nothing but Tighty Whities that it dawned on Caan that this was *supposed* to be a comedy.

The edit was tough. Frustrating his producers yet again, Anderson delivered a rough cut that seemed to ramble on forever. There were gorgeous scenes that had no purpose. He took convincing to cut it into something manageable. Worse was to come. Unthinkably, the

Sundance festival rejected the film, their schedule already crowded with eccentric comedies. The project was starting to seem like an outcast.

Then *Bottle Rocket* received the worse test screening scores of any film put before an audience by Sony. Anderson ruefully recalled that before the screening the studio claimed to have had no expectations. Afterwards their 'feelings'[33] were confirmed. People had walked out in droves and finally Anderson went with them. Serious re-editing was demanded, as well as reshoots. In a process of what they saw as damage limitation, Sony postponed the release date and cancelled the premiere, eventually tossing the film onto a few screens in January 1996 with negligible marketing.

Anderson's confidence had been at 'an all-time high'[34] during the making of the film, but he was shattered by the release. Wilson seriously considered enlisting in the Marines.

Above: Landing Caan was pure serendipity; he and Anderson shared an agent. The director's first choice, Bill Murray, didn't even bother to read the script.

Right: Caan was a livewire on set, but he enthralled the young filmmakers with tales from his illustrious career – a legacy *Bottle Rocket* was investing in.

But Brooks offered hope. He considered the film well directed. That voice he had sensed was growing louder. Studio qualms aside, the critics were getting Anderson. Brooks had arranged a series of screenings around town and the word began to spread. This guy had something, if no one quite yet could put a finger on what (they still struggle to fathom him).

Kenneth Turan, influential critic at the *Los Angeles Times*, was a significant early supporter, who thought it was 'inexplicable' the film had been turned down by Sundance. Here was a unique new sensibility, both mischievous and heartfelt. 'A confident, eccentric debut about a trio of shambling and guileless friends who become the Candides of crime, *Rocket* feels particularly refreshing because it never compromises on its delicate deadpan sensibility.'[35]

'These were pioneers of comic naiveté,' agreed Desson Howe in the *Washington Post*: 'They're purely interested in the way events can unfold – no matter how strange.'[36]

With *Bottle Rocket*, standard resolutions are out of reach. There is an open-ended mystery to everything. The style is only beginning to take shape. This is Anderson's loosest movie. Sartorially too. Informal black-and-white photographs from the set show Anderson as thin as a scarecrow, still in jeans and John Lennon-style specs, with his hair cut boyishly short. It is as if he and his films grew neater by the year.

Dallas-based critic Matt Zoller Seitz, chief disciple at the altar of Anderson since reviewing the *Bottle Rocket* short at the USA Film Festival (its debut), regards the feature as having showed the city in a 'uniquely personal and artful way.'[37] Which is a fair summary of the Anderson mindset. The appreciation of light and space and architecture transformed Dallas into a world of

Above: Luke Wilson was nervous about the romantic elements of his part. Nevertheless, his scenes with the Paraguayan maid Inez (Mexican actress Lumi Cavazos) are among the most sweetly effective in the entire film.

Above: Luke Wilson as Anthony is ostensibly the film's hero, if such things count. He is a sweet but damaged soul, a type that would be found drifting throughout Anderson's canon.

enchantment ... nothing like *Dallas*, the gaudy eighties soap opera, which had conditioned the world to think of the Texan city as a prefabricated sprawl of skyscrapers and ranches. Anderson treated Dallas as if it was Paris, inflected with Pop Art and loneliness.

What he revealed, if not yet perfectly, was a vision. Here was a director for whom the overall feel was as important as any particular detail. Like George Lucas, he was a builder of bizarre worlds, but grounded in emotional reality.

A short word on references: this early stage is a good time to explain the extent to which Anderson is a cultural magpie. All his films are like stamp collections of filmic, literary, artistic and musical citations that direct our

attention to Anderson's thinking. He is, it goes without saying, an ardent cinephile, growing his work from the rich soil of the medium. For *Bottle Rocket*, Anderson charged his crew to always bear in mind not only French influences, but also the sensuous cityscapes of Bernardo Bertolucci's spy thriller *The Conformist*. Yeoman even had still-frame images next his viewfinder.

But that Tarantino-like shoot-from-the-hip referencing goes one stage further. Increasingly, Anderson's films will themselves literally become collections – each frame populated with a treasure trove of props and decor in which the characters are embedded and reflected.

Inherent in both the story of these wide-eyed fools and in the ill-formed

clay of the filmmakers was the promise of something: a dream of the future and adventure.

It was too late to save *Bottle Rocket* from box office ignominy (it made less than $1 million), but given its miserly release the film didn't really have a chance. And out of it would emerge a cult. No less a luminary than Scorsese ensured the film a rebirth on DVD by naming it in his top ten of 1996 and installing Anderson among the vanguard of a new generation of filmmakers.

'Here was a picture without a trace of cynicism,' wrote Scorsese, describing the film as a rarity. He found himself drawn to its delicacy, what he felt was human in the story. 'A group of young guys that think that their lives have to be filled with risk and danger in order to be real. They don't know that it's okay simply to be who they are.'[38]

He drew a likeness to the work of Leo McCarey (screwball director of *Duck Soup* and *The Awful Truth*) and the great French master Jean Renoir, which shared that same intimate bond with the characters. Anderson seemed to care deeply about these people. Scorsese was too polite to draw the clear parallels with his own *Mean Streets*: the loose camber of friendships, the yearning for purpose, and the championing of anarchic youth.

This was an era where talent could still shout louder than box office. Hip young things were in demand, and both Anderson and Wilson found their careers skyrocketing.

Above: Owen Wilson as Anthony's BFF Dignan clutching a titular bottle rocket (a cheap firework). Dignan's nervous, hyper-verbal tics laid down another template for characters to come.

RUSHMORE

For his second film, Wes Anderson turned for inspiration to his schooldays at a prim, private Houston academy. The rarefied coming of age that ensued is the tragicomedy against which all his other films are judged

Even with only one film to his name, Wes Anderson was already behaving like an auteur, driven solely by his own mysterious whims. *Bottle Rocket* barely scraping a dime at the box office was almost a boon. It made him hip. And after Martin Scorsese declared his allegiance, membership of the Anderson fan club was on the up-and-up among Hollywood's topmost echelons (i.e. the money men). He was swiftly established as that rarity – the idiosyncratic filmmaker indulged by the studios. He was being worn like a badge of credibility.

There might be numerous flavours to choose from in the chocolate box of Anderson's imagination, but when he finishes one movie and contemplates the next, he usually knows exactly where he is going. Right now, he was set on enrolling in *Rushmore*, the story of a precocious fifteen-year-old schoolboy with emotional issues and his relationship with a vaguely suicidal middle-aged steel magnate. Which screamed box office gold to precisely no one, but there were plenty of willing takers.

As with *Bottle Rocket*, the idea had been one of the treatments accompanying an application to a film school Anderson never attended (also included were preliminary notes on *The Life Aquatic with Steve Zissou*). Likewise, he would write the script in collaboration with Owen Wilson,

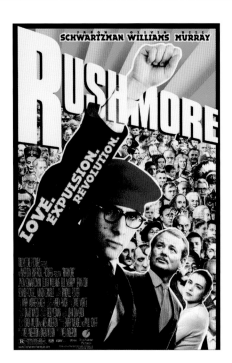

Above: *Rushmore* – now viewed as Wes Anderson's breakthrough movie – is, if anything, even more personal than his offbeat debut.

Right: Jason Schwartzman as prep-school misfit Max Fischer was the exact opposite of how Anderson had pictured the part. He was the perfect spiritual fit. It was also something about the way he walked.

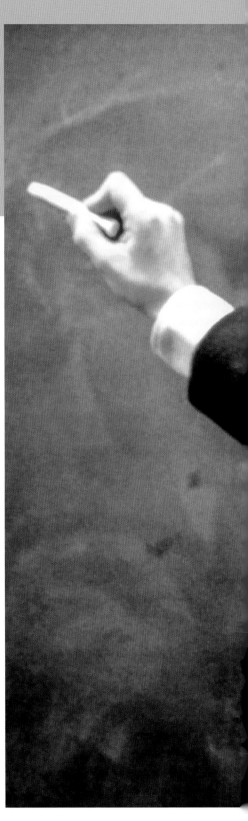

and they had begun pooling their thoughts on the second movie before filming the first. Anderson depends on collaboration; all but one of his films has been written with a partner. He likes to talk and walk a script through before writing it down (a process which involves a lot of scraps of paper). He also likes the company. Writing is such a lonely business compared to the communal buzz of the movie set.

Generically speaking, *Rushmore* was to be his 'school movie,'[1] in the raucous British tradition of Lindsay Anderson (*if....*), yet infused with the sad-sack charms of Charles M. Schulz's beloved loser Charlie Brown from the *Peanuts* strips and cartoons (whose understated poignancy has long given succour to Anderson) – and, instinctively, a helping of Wes Anderson's schooldays, as well as those of Wilson, who was thrown out of prep school for cheating in his geometry exam. Further down the checklist of film quotations are intergenerational romantic comedy *Harold And Maude*, the cynical tykes from 1976 baseball perennial *The Bad News Bears* (a set text when it comes to Anderson's gatherings

of pre-emptively aged youngsters), and, as we shall see, big, talky thrillers featuring men in peril.

For many Andersonites, *Rushmore* is maybe even the fullest expression of his talents. Biographer Matt Zoller Seitz thinks of it as one of history's 'few perfect films.'[2] It is certainly here where the style takes root. Not just the patchwork quilt of allusions and geometry set of camera tricks, but such merriments as a symbolic wraparound device (in this case, the parting of theatrical curtains actually filmed on set), witty captions (inspired by Jean-Luc Godard), compendiums of props, costumes and songs, an unimpressable female at the pointiest corner of a love triangle, that elusive yet piquant tone somewhere between sad-funny and funny-sad, and Bill Murray.

Rushmore is Anderson coming of age. Wilson's good looks and wiseacre routine had started him on a procession of roles in dumb mainstream fare like *Anaconda*, *Armageddon,* and *The Cable Guy* (where he is credited, to his best friend's amusement, as 'obnoxious boyfriend'). Though his position as

Anderson's dance partner would wax and wane over the coming years, working with his friend remained the priority. Confronting a 'looming fear'[3] that they might never be able to write anything else, as the dust settled on *Bottle Rocket* they went back to finish school.

Rumours persist that Wilson has a heavily disguised cameo in the finished *Rushmore*, but it's not true. Beyond the script, he can be found in school photographs on the wall of a classroom. Luke Wilson (also making hay as an actor) takes a brief role, in surgical scrubs, as an affable boyfriend.

Anderson had met producer Barry Mendel in Los Angeles while trying to write *Bottle Rocket*. They were a good fit. Mendel shared his deadpan view on life, but he also came with a Hollywood Rolodex. Through his ministrations the *Rushmore* script was developed with seed money from New Line Cinema (a division of Warner Bros. with an indie complexion), whose tolerance for quirk was finally broken when Anderson pitched it to them as *Serpico* in a prep school. Undeterred, Mendel boldly put the rights up for auction and four studios

made an offer. They went with Disney – through their more adult arm Touchstone Pictures – when chairman Joe Roth turned out to be another member of the secret society of *Bottle Rocket* fans. He also offered nearly double the budget of Anderson's debut, though at $9 million this hardly represented a great gamble.

A brief interlude on the whole indie thing: for obvious reasons – the nature of his films, the cut of his corduroy suits, his taste for French movies, his middling box office – Anderson tends to be catalogued with the whole Miramax-indie revolution that crashed the multiplexes of the nineties. You know the crowd: Todds Haynes and Solondz, Paul Thomas Anderson, Spike Jonze, Quentin Tarantino and his fast-talking crew, and (at the time) Steven Soderbergh. In fairness, their success had made Anderson's rise more likely. On the other hand, it's worth clarifying that Anderson has made every one of his films within the embrace of the studio system.

Ironically, he's also far less ironic than his so-called peers. His films might be heightened collages of references and jokes, but they are sincere. He is not remote from his characters, he sees himself in them. *Rushmore*, he liked to say, was 'pure of heart.'[4]

Above: The beginning of a beautiful friendship: Anderson finally got his wish when muse-in-the-making Bill Murray accepted the role of Max's 'vaguely suicidal' mentor-partner-love rival Herman Blume.

What Disney had bought into was the story of Max Fischer (Jason Schwartzman), Class of '01 at the Rushmore Academy, a Houston preparatory in quiet decline. Fifteen going on fifty and a hopeless Renaissance man, Max falls head over heels for hot first-grade teacher Rosemary Cross (Olivia Williams). He really doesn't see a problem with the age difference. She, on the other hand, really does.

There are things about Max you should know. He thinks he's quite the cat, or at any rate talks that way in intense, hyper-verbal brainwaves like Dignan in *Bottle Rocket*. He's a very poor student, but a *tour de force* on the extracurricular scene. We are treated to a bravura sixty-two-second 'yearbook' montage that surely sums up Anderson's idea of swell pursuits: French Club President, Stamp & Coin Collecting Vice-President, Calligraphy Club, 2nd Chorale Choirmaster, Beekeeper President etc. And Max has roped local businessman Herman Blume (the effortlessly dismayed Bill Murray) into funding the construction of a school aquarium.

Things get tricky when the unhappily married Herman begins his own attempts to woo Rosemary. 'I was in love with her first,'[5] pouts the infuriated Max as battle commences. One other thing, beneath Max's unquenchable bravado is a well of unexpressed grief for his dead mother.

It's too easy to read Max as Wes. While the corridors and lawns of Rushmore Academy may be a match for Anderson's Houston alma mater St. John's School (largely because that is exactly where he shot it), for the most part he had better grades. Max is flunking everything.

Then again, Anderson did put on plays – just as Max, the self-styled head of the Max Fischer Players, mounts

elaborate, gimcrack productions like miniature Anderson movies, each adapted from the screenwriters' favourite tough guy pictures. These include Sidney Lumet's study of police corruption, *Serpico*, complete with loft apartment, elevated train and pupils doing salty New York accents. And Anderson did have a crush on an older teacher.

Conversely, Schwartzman, raven-haired scion of the Coppola clan (his mother is actress Talia Shire, sister of Francis Ford Coppola, director of *The Godfather*) had been, by his own confession, 'deeply' in love with his nanny. Add Wilson's disciplinary foibles and we can consider Max a conglomerate of angst.

In the range of 1,800 hopefuls tried out for the part from all corners of America, Canada and England. Anderson had fourteen casting directors at work, determined not to end up with some pampered offspring of a famous Hollywood dynasty. Which was exactly what he got.

Schwartzman had no aspiration to be an actor. He was seventeen and

Above: Max (Schwartzman) alongside object-of-his-confused-affections Miss Cross (Olivia Williams). As soon as he met British actress Williams, it made perfect sense to Anderson for the character to be British, rendering her more aloof and fragile.

Opposite: Max's montage of towering extracurricular achievements, including publishing Rushmore newspaper the *Yankee Review*, provide an insight into the kind of multifarious interests that feed Anderson's universe.

played drums. His only experience to date, as pointed out by his Uncle Francis, was performing in his cousin's plays at family gatherings. Case in point, it was cousin Sofia Coppola who talked him into meeting the *Rushmore* casting agent, who talked him into meeting Anderson.

As Schwartzman walked in the room there was an instant rapport, partly because they were both so young, partly because they really admired one another's footwear (the actor: Converse sandals; the director: green New Balances with red reflectors), partly because of a mutual love of L.A. rock band Weezer, and partly because Schwartzman had turned up to the audition like many of his rivals in a navy blazer, only he had added a homemade Rushmore Academy insignia. Such is the way to Anderson's heart.

Even around Hollywood, the young director would affect a preppy out-of-towner ensemble of blazers and trousers too small for his gangly six-foot-one frame. He looked more likely to help with your homework than make a movie. With the passing of time, this sartorial novelty has eased off into bespoke russet suits and asparagus green ties (or vice versa).

In his head, Anderson he had been looking for 'a fifteen-year-old Mick Jagger,'[6] but he was thrilled with a stocky, stony-faced Schwartzman. 'The movie, in the end – well, it's his face and it's his voice. And his personality is very distinctive.'[7]

Coming to terms with the fact he was an actor after all (he has now featured in six different Andersonian fables, part of a second extended family), Schwartzman takes full charge of the character's overgrown perspective on the world and never lets the façade crack. Beneath Groucho Marx eyebrows and clownish specs he barely changes expression. There were technical issues: Schwartzman, who tended toward the hirsute even as a teenager, was shaved and waxed to ensure he appeared suitably callow, especially in the wrestling scene. 'Yeah and the hands,'[8] he winced in recollection.

Above: Williams and Schwartzman, Max and Miss Rose, stand by on set. That red beret would become a regular sartorial choice among Anderson's disconsolate youth.

Left: Seymour Cassel as Max's genial pop Bert and Schwartzman lope around behind the scenes. Cassel was another of those actors chosen by Anderson in honour of their great seventies film pedigree.

Left: Dustin Hoffman in the famous publicity shot from *The Graduate,* from which Anderson would draw the older-woman motif and the sense of dislocation in his young hero.

Max has a touch of the prodigy about him, like his namesake and chess wonder Bobby Fischer. He is trying to uphold the wilting Rushmore tradition. Anderson's films come steeped in this nostalgia for fabled yesterdays: think of Gustave H. reminiscing about the heyday of *The Grand Budapest Hotel.* They are characters and worlds and a director sliding backwards in time. Which is why they are timeless.

Everything to Max is playacting. He's acting the lothario, grandly in love with a much older woman (and potential mother replacement). There is an echo of Dustin Hoffman in *The Graduate* in his body language, a sense of stifled energy.

One of the many joys of *Rushmore* is that while wholly objectionable, Max remains endearing. We root for him. For he's acting the rich kid too. He's kind of heroically antiheroic. He made it to Rushmore on a scholarship and fibs to his wealthy classmates that his father is a neurosurgeon when in fact he's the local barber. Seymour Cassel, who had worked with the great John Cassavetes in the seventies, plays Max's shamefully humble but contented pop with the exact same crew cut and spectacles as *Peanuts* creator Schulz, whose father also happened to be a barber.

'I like characters that are trying to realize their projects,' explained Anderson, playing

out his own quixotic journey in their indomitability in the face of naysayers. 'I mean, building an aquarium, putting on a Vietnam play with explosions on the stage is crazy – but Max does that.'[9]

Max, like the *Bottle Rocket* boys, is chasing a miniaturist rendition of the American Dream. They might be overreaching, but they are anything but slackers. And it's never simply to be rich. Even those with the loot, like Herman Blume, yearn for adventure.

Fundamental to all Anderson plots are people with 'unrealistic ambitions.'[10]

Rushmore is the first of many Anderson trips to that border country where 'young hearts want to be old and old hearts want to be young.'[11] The phenomenon of adults (mostly Murray) slumping back into childish ways, while the kids try out maturity. As with Blume and Max, they tend to meet halfway. These two make for the perfectly odd couple. One is a virtuoso of hopelessness, the other wears optimism like a suit of armour.

Murray had fallen into Anderson's orbit by fluke. The director was naturally a huge fan. That symphony of droll perfected in *The National Lampoon Radio Hour* and *Saturday Night Live* before souring the gee-whizz high concepts of *Ghostbusters*, *Scrooged* and *Groundhog Day* to perfection had made the actor one of the biggest comedy stars of the eighties and nineties. This was despite Murray doing his darnedest to confound the notion of stardom. The fifth of nine children of a mailroom clerk mother and lumber salesman father from Wilmette, Illinois (near Chicago), he was a bottle rocket celebrity as liable to wrestle an interviewer to the ground as answer a question. He prided himself on being unobtainable via regular Hollywood channels. He rarely responded to his agent's entreaties. It could take months to get a reply.

Anderson had several backups in mind only because he was resigned to not getting his heart's desire to mine the less obviously nuts side Murray had shown in *Mad Dog and Glory*, *Ed Wood* and *Razor's Edge*.

Yet Murray was at a crossroads. Recent sourpuss star vehicles *Larger Than Life* and *The Man Who Knew Too Little* had flopped badly. There was a growing hunger to be more serious. He needed Anderson as much as Anderson needed him. Through his regular appearances in Anderson's films, from

leading man to cameo (it's now an 'automatic yes'[12] whenever he calls), Murray assembled a rich second act for his career that mixed his asinine worldliness with vulnerability and encompassed an Oscar nomination for Sofia Coppola's *Lost in Translation*.

Revitalized in misery, he has become, as Anthony Lane of *The New Yorker* put it, 'the most singular presence in American cinema.'[13] Murray's expressive mug, as round and pocked as the surface of the Moon, is a map of human bafflement and sorrow. The genius of Murray is that his pokerfaced melancholy is so indefinable, root cause doesn't even apply. Beginning with Herman Blume, he summons up an aura of despair that is existential. We can but laugh.

Fortunately, Murray's agent had been another of those to get *Bottle Rocket* (though Murray had revealed no interest in playing Mr. Henry), and urged his client to read the new script. The character clearly touched a chord, for Murray got back to Anderson within a week, agreeing to work for scale – he termed it 'pro bono'[14] – with a smaller slice of the profits than was usual. His only stipulation was to start earlier than scheduled rather than wait.

In subsequent interviews Murray suggested he is often drawn to the chance to 'go down with the guys who don't have a chance.'[15] Which was a backhanded compliment, but that deal helped make the film happen.

On Murray's first day on set, Anderson whispered his instructions

Left: Herman had been written with Murray in mind, and thankfully the notoriously diffident Murray was won over by the script, claiming it was among the best he had ever read.

Right: All's well that ends well – the school prom grants Max a more age-appropriate girlfriend in Sara Tanaka's Margaret Yang. Incidentally, the scene where Max lifts up Margaret's glasses is an exact replica of the one in *Rocky* where Sylvester Stallone does the same with Talia Shire, Schwartzman's mother.

Below: Murray and Schwartzman as the oddest of odd couples, Herman and Max – in Anderson's mind they mark the perfect intersection of an old guy reverting to youth and a young man old before his time.

to the star, fearful of ruffling feathers. Murray instantly made a big deal out of deferring to the young director, a completely different temperature to James Caan. He was having a ball, hauling equipment with the crew, more court jester than diva. He even presented Anderson with a blank cheque to fund a helicopter shot when Disney baulked at the $75,000 cost (the shot was dropped in any case, but Anderson is still in possession of that cheque should an emergency arise).

Then Blume fitted the actor like a worn suit (he wears the same one throughout). On the downslope of a marriage, the local plutocrat is the model of American wealth in tailspin who finds his sagging spirit stirred by both Max and Rosemary. So beguiling was Murray's depiction of what is essentially depression – but always with a sense of impending mischief – Touchstone brought forward the release of the film in the hopes of landing him an Oscar nomination for Supporting Actor (it didn't catch, the fools). 'If you just watch his eyes,' said Mendel, 'you can understand the entire story.'[16]

Rich Uncle Pennybags, better known as the mascot for the game Monopoly, was a spiritual forebear for Herman. 'Well, he sells steel,'[17] said Anderson, whose working title for *Rushmore* was *The Tycoon*. As written, Herman was in the concrete business, but they found a foundry that supplied steel pipes to the Houston area and switched for the aesthetics. Anderson loved the sparks flying in the background. Those surreal, European touches often carry inexpressible significance. Blume's office, raised on steel stilts, is the first set he ever built. From hereon, he began constructing his worlds from scratch, reality rarely sufficient for his requirements.

Now what of Miss Cross, a rose between dorks, the pretty first-grade teacher with her own knapsack of sorrow? She's lost a husband, the oceanographer Edward Appleby, and sleeps in his bedroom at his parents' home where model airplanes still hang from the ceiling. That's part of the problem. Rose can see Edward in Max's adventurous spirit and puppy-dog eyes.

Anderson only thought how perfect it would be to have Rosemary Cross be English once he met Williams, the London-born, Royal-Shakespeare-Company-trained actress rallying after the dismal performance of her futuristic debut, *The Postman*. Being English seemed to make her more precious. To Max she requires courting. 'We should have written it that way … It just made sense,'[18] said Anderson. Williams had to get used to the director's back-to-front way of presenting things. All his instructions seemed to be contradictions: 'I want you to be serious, but laughing.'[19]

Incidentally, the aquarium, which Max is building and Blume funding to woo Rosemary, points us toward an autobiographical detail Anderson tends to slalom past in interview. He adored the documentaries of famous French oceanographer Jacques Cousteau as a child and Max is first drawn to Rosemary via her late husband's book of Cousteau's nautical adventures donated to the Rushmore library. It was also advance notice of where Anderson would head next but one.

While the three characters remain front and centre of the story (and most shots) there are memorable side attractions, not least Mason Gamble (formerly *Dennis the Menace*) as Max's stoic sidekick and conscience Dirk (or as Anderson informed him, the 'Linus' to his Charlie Brown), and Brian Cox as Rushmore's exasperated head and Max's nemesis Mr. Guggenheim. Anderson cast the burly Scottish actor largely because he had played Hannibal Lecktor in *Manhunter*, then dressed him up in hunting tweeds.

Opposite: Miss Cross (Williams), revealed to be Rosemary, and Herman (Murray) share an intimate moment. Each of the three main characters is defined and connected to the others by a sense of loss.

Right: Brian Cox as the long-suffering headmaster Dr. Nelson Guggenheim was cast on the strength of his performance as icy genius Hannibal Lecktor in Michael Mann's movie, *Manhunter*.

Below: Max and sidekick Dirk Calloway, played by Mason Gamble, who had been Dennis the Menace in the adaptation of Hank Ketcham's comic strip about a mischief-prone boy – another inspiration for Max.

CONTENTMENT PROVIDER

A guide to visual motifs, or Wes Anderson bingo

Works of Art: Paintings, sculptures, books, plays, films (within the film), and documentaries all feature as major plot devices. In *The Grand Budapest Hotel*, 'Boy with Apple' by fictional Renaissance dauber Johannes Van Hoytl the Younger (in actuality it was painted by British artist Michael Taylor) counts as the MacGuffin.

Food: There is a lot of eating to be done in Anderson's films. As a taster, try: the exquisite Courtesan au Chocolat (*The Grand Budapest Hotel*), Red Remarkable Apples (*Fantastic Mr. Fox*), savoury travel snacks (*The Darjeeling Limited*), a compartmentalized Thanksgiving TV dinner (*Rushmore*), and stolen espressos (*The Life Aquatic with Steve Zissou*).

Khaki: Be it suits (*Fantastic Mr. Fox*), cowboy outfits (*The Royal Tenenbaums*), scout uniforms (*Moonrise Kingdom*), Margot's underwear (*The Royal Tenenbaums*), or Raleigh's drab housecoat (ditto), shades of brown persist in the costumes. See also: the sartorial choices of the director.

Berets: Maybe it's a French thing, or an artistic thing, but among many styles of headwear, berets do stand out. Max wears a scarlet number in *Rushmore*, while Suzy in *Moonrise Kingdom* has a raspberry-hued version.

Moustaches: Fine facial hair is common throughout the Andersonian oeuvre, and moustaches are a particular mark of (attempted) refinement and class. Namely: Herman in *Rushmore*, Royal in *The Royal Tenenbaums*, Ned in *The Life Aquatic with Steve Zissou*, Jack in *The Darjeeling Limited*, Gustave H. in *The Grand Budapest Hotel*, etc.

Binoculars: We often catch characters gazing through binoculars (Suzy in *Moonrise Kingdom* is a real peeping tom). Since Anderson is a director obsessed with detail, perhaps this is a subliminal instruction to pay close attention.

Lists: There is always one character who keeps a firm tab on proceedings by making lists, notes, itineraries, and generally planning stuff like a director would (such as Dignan in *Bottle Rocket*, Francis in *The Darjeeling Limited*, Zero in *The Grand Budapest Hotel*). This also covers maps and diagrams.

Futura: From *Bottle Rocket* onwards, Anderson's titles, captions and (often) marketing material stuck to the typeface Futura (bold). This could be in tribute to Stanley Kubrick, who loved Futura Extra Bold, or maybe simply because it is rather neat. It was only when he got to *Moonrise Kingdom* that Anderson brought in a florid new font, specially designed for the film. When it came to the pre-war world of *The Grand Budapest Hotel*, he turned to the more classical Archer font.

Outmoded Audio Equipment: Whatever the era, whatever the reason – pure nostalgia, analogue fetish, love of big switches – Anderson has his characters use big old-fashioned tape recorders, Dictaphones, plastic telephones, headphones, and record players. This includes pretty much all the rattletrap tech on board the *Belafonte* in *The Life Aquatic with Steve Zissou*.

Modes of Transport: Planes, trains, automobiles, boats, submarines, diggers, go-karts, motorbikes (with and without sidecars), bicycles, and ski lifts. For a man fixed in his ways, Anderson likes to stay on the move. Every one of his films features the characters utilizing various forms of transport, and by *The Grand Budapest Hotel* there are chase sequences. Both *The Life Aquatic with Steve Zissou* (on board a ship), and *The Darjeeling Limited* (on board a train), are defined by their mode of transport.

Left: Tony Revolori applies his pencil moustache in *The Grand Budapest Hotel*, a literal mark of distinction.

Left: Anderson marvelled at how Schwartzman looked nothing like Max in real life. With those glasses and the carefully sculpted Groucho Marx eyebrows he transformed into this whole other person.

Shooting from 22 November 1997 for a little over two months, *Rushmore* was literally a world Anderson knew by heart. They were filming in his footsteps. 'I'd gone to the school,' he said. 'So when we were working on the script, I was picturing, "This is the corner, this is behind the air-conditioning unit, next to the thing here ... " And we shot it next to the air-conditioning unit.'[20]

While Anderson was there, St. John's actually held a ten-year reunion, but he was unable to attend, as he was too busy filming a movie down the corridor.

The first instinct had been to film in New England in the fall and send up the dappled imagery of *Dead Poets Society*. He just couldn't find a school to fit the one in his head. He found something close in England, but that was too far to go. 'Then my mother sent pictures of my own school,' he laughed, 'and I realized that's what I was trying to find all along.'[21]

The uniform that Max wears – blue shirt, khaki pants – is the original St. John's outfit. Though the navy blazer is an affectation. When Max finally gets thrown out of Rushmore (those grades!

That spell in jail! The unapproved aquarium being built on the baseball diamond!) he tumbles down the food chain to Grover Cleveland High, as played by Lamar, the school Anderson's father went to. It was literally across the road but made to look as desolate as a prison.

The hermetically sealed world of Rushmore Academy sits at the centre of an Andersonian Venn diagram where factual detail overlaps with fictional fancy. You would never place it in Houston. 'We wanted it to feel kind of like a fable, I guess,' he observed, 'a little unreal.'[22] This was the way Max sees Rushmore, like a Powell & Pressburger movie, or Scorsese's *The Age of Innocence*, or Truffaut's *Two English Girls*. All of which, Anderson had his heads of department watch before setting out.

He also distributed a set of postcards featuring paintings by Hans Holbein the Elder and Agnolo Bronzino. 'There's a colour scheme in them,'[23] he explained, and that transition into Gothic. With *Bottle Rocket* it had been all about the Hockneys. Here he wanted those subdued, old-world colours.

The layering continued. French photographer Jacques Henri Lartigue was a child prodigy with a camera in his hands at six, and the brief shot of Max in goggles on the go-kart during the montage of school clubs is a reference to his shot 'Zissou's bobsled with wheels, after the bend by the gate, Rouzat, August 1908.' The original can be seen on the wall behind Max's desk. And the referential threads run on into later films, especially *The Life Aquatic with Steve Zissou*.

A brief word on set decoration: Anderson's romantic refitting of the world into elegant tableaux has expanded into a defining style. 'He loves the idea that he can really create every bit of the image that's on the screen,'[24] appreciated Jeremy Dawson, producer of such carousels as *The Darjeeling Limited* and *Moonrise Kingdom*. As we shall see, everything in the frame carries a just-so symbolic point. Even if a coffee cup is only fleetingly glimpsed in the background, Dawson noted, Anderson will have it made in advance exactly like one he saw in a New York restaurant. He thinks of this as his handwriting.

'This is what Wes Anderson does,' says Sophie Monks Kaufman in her excellent monograph *Wes Anderson*. 'He wills magic parallel universes into being, using all he has to create stories free from all but his artistic values.'[25]

Working from his own rigorous storyboards, Anderson plotted out each sequence with tidy precision. Nothing was left to chance. His methods are defiantly anti-slacker. Like Max, but to less misguided ends, he is inexhaustibly ingenious. The confidence had flooded back.

It is in *Rushmore* we see the fruition of the signature Anderson ninety-degree angle framing or Planimetric Shot.

A concise history of the Planimetric Shot: as classified by the art historian Heinrich Wölfflin (a real person, as it happens), this distinctive shot was cultivated by the likes of Kubrick, Godard, Ozu, and Buster Keaton (another directorial cake mix for an Andersonian gateau). This painterly method involves the camera standing perpendicular to a background in front of which the actors can be arranged like clothes on a line or a police line up. In Anderson's hands, a single character is often perfectly centred and looking outwards past the camera.

The first thing cinematographer Robert Yeoman does on their latest film is figure out how to centre the character in the frame; he then waits for his director to smile.

Opposite: Schwartzman's Max in Tom Cruise aviator shades, a devoted member of the Piper Cub Club. The lightweight Piper Cub airplane is an American classic, and its standard chrome yellow paintwork is known as Cub Yellow, another passing detail that feels significant.

The confounding tone, so downbeat yet effervescent, serious and funny, is guided by the music. Anderson planned to have the film scored entirely by The Kinks for the British vibe (they wore blazers), but that didn't work out. Instead he uses a playlist from across British pop music of the sixties and seventies, a teen sound both anarchic and melodic that kind of summed up Max's manic esprit. Songs like *Oh Yoko* by John Lennon and *Ooh La La* by Ronnie Wood were played on set, enabling Anderson to give scenes a jaunty rhythm.

The film finishes in grand style with Max's operatic Vietnam play – comprised of explosions and flamethrowers and homages to *Apocalypse Now* (directed by Schwartzman's uncle, of course), *Platoon*, and *The Deer Hunter* ... with Max, the star, done up like Robert De Niro. Blume watches on with tears in his eyes, a Vietnam veteran. There follows a dance, modelled precisely on *A Charlie Brown Christmas*.

Released on 11 December 1998, the critics were bouncing (though they again struggled to pinpoint the genre), even if a wider audience was still scratching its collective head. However, a box office return of $17 million was a darn sight better than *Bottle Rocket*. As Murray sagely predicted, *Rushmore* has become a beloved American movie. Though not quite everyone was onboard.

Let us end this chapter with another salutary story. Herein Anderson is desperate for the great Pauline Kael to see his new movie. The small, snappy doyenne of critics from *The New Yorker* was responsible for shaping his tastes. So, channelling Max's intrepid self-aggrandisement, he arranges a special screening of *Rushmore* at a multiplex near her Massachusetts home. Thus begins a passage of comic awkwardness and disillusionment worthy of one of his films. Let us bypass the fact that by picking up the elderly critic in his

car, Anderson is forced to risk double-parking so he can walk her into the cinema. 'My God, you're just a kid,'[26] she remarks, opening the front door to look upon this director who has brought cookies to share during the film.

Let us instead cut to Kael's cluttered clapboard house *after* the screening. The place is so crammed with books and boxes they have to turn sideways to navigate their way to a seat. Kael keeps things honest. 'I don't know what you've got here, Wes,' she smarts. 'Did the people who gave you the money read the script?'[27]

'I don't know if it was really her bag,'[28] Anderson reflected later.

Kael also mentions that *Bottle Rocket* seemed 'thrown together' – and besides, 'Wes Anderson is a terrible name for a movie director.'[29]

The poorly baptized director was left deflated, but like in all of Anderson's stories, pilgrimages are never fruitless. While there, Kael opened a closet to reveal a treasure chamber of her books perfectly arranged in their original print runs. She invited him to take whatever he wished. Fighting down the urge to grab a complete set, Anderson selected two first editions, which he had her sign before driving away.

Moreover, in his next film, the saga of a soured clan of New Yorkers called *The Royal Tenenbaums*, Anderson has undependable patriarch Royal (Gene Hackman) deliver a pitiless assessment of his eleven-year-old daughter Margot's play about talking animals. 'It didn't seem believable to me,'[30] he shrugs.

In the one after, *The Life Aquatic with Steve Zissou*, narcissistic oceanographer Steve Zissou (Bill Murray) reveals that the library of his research ship, the *Belafonte*, has a 'complete first edition set of *The Life Aquatic Companion Series*,'[31] his own publication.

Max would approve.

THE ROYAL TENENBAUMS

For his third film, Wes Anderson departed for New York to survey the wreckage of a highly dysfunctional family of geniuses. An uproarious tragedy – more ambitious, starrier and weirder than ever

'We are all Tenenbaums,'[1] claimed critic Matt Zoller Seitz. Which sounds a little far-fetched, given Wes Anderson's extended clan of rich and self-obsessed New York misfits have excelled in many fields: professional tennis, finance, chemistry, novels, plays, neurology, and manic depression. After the relative success of *Rushmore*, Anderson brought forth a comedy of success among relatives, and its aftermath. The tensions of the Tenenbaums are designed to give us pause over the complex relationships we might have with our own parents, siblings and other animals. It's all the stuff you don't talk about, wrapped in one neat movie package. Furthermore, we are catching up with the Tenenbaums in a real slump.

As with *Rushmore* before it, Anderson had been jotting down notes for his New York family saga since before *Bottle Rocket*. To an extent the story had been circling in his mind since his parents' divorce. That is one of the reasons why, for all the film's jazzy absurdity, the traumas feel so real. Mild-mannered matriarch Etheline Tenenbaum (Anjelica Huston) is an archaeologist just like Anderson's mother – we'll come back to this. For all the Swiss clockwork precision, *The Royal Tenenbaums* is a film about the collateral damage done when marriages fall apart. It was like a bomb going off, said

Anderson, remembering the splintering of his own family, 'or maybe imploding.'[2]

The screenplay took shape over a year. It was written, once again, in partnership with Owen Wilson, and they began with the idea of a generation of child geniuses who have failed as grown-ups. 'We had a good idea of the characters and who they were long before there was any story,'[3] said Anderson, and the characters began to dictate the plot. Especially the father figure, who moved to the forefront of the screenplay when he 'started to make things happen in the story.'[4]

Fundamentally, this is the story of what happens when the paterfamilias,

Above: Bill Murray as sullen neurologist Raleigh St. Clair, the next in line of his Andersonian misery-guts. Note the blackboard sketch of the self-same character initialled by the director himself.

Opposite: *The Royal Tenenbaums*, with its big names and a cool New York backdrop, would still daringly pirouette between comedy and tragedy.

Royal Tenenbaum (a marvellous Gene Hackman, channelling a variety of Mephistophelian bonhomie), root cause of ninety percent of prevailing Tenenbaum dysfunction, returns home to set things right. Royal has been living in a hotel for twenty-two years, having split, but not yet divorced, from Etheline. Royal's return will stir up a lot of unwanted flashbacks – each character cultivating their own briar patch of subplot – filling us in on the fact that his specific genius was for wayward parenthood. We'll come back to this.

When Etheline contemplates a marriage proposal from dapper, reliable family accountant Henry Sherman (author of the wonderfully entitled *Accounting for Everything*, and played by Danny Glover, his look modelled on former UN Secretary-General Kofi Annan), Royal concocts a fake stomach cancer and inveigles himself back into the family home and the entangled lives of his three children, who are gradually reoccupying their former

bedrooms. On the second floor is chemical industry financier Chas (Ben Stiller), who has become paranoid and overprotective of his two sons since the death of his wife in a plane crash. On the third is adopted Margot (Gwyneth Paltrow), author of such plays as *Nakedness Tonight* and *Static Electricity*, absconded from a malfunctioning marriage and stymied by writer's block. In the attic should be Royal's favourite, Richie (Luke Wilson), the tennis pro who froze on the European circuit, but he's currently all at sea – we'll come back to this.

Across the road dwells Richie's best friend Eli Cash (Owen Wilson, also back in front of the camera), best-selling author of preposterous Westerns (such as *Old Custer*, which reads like a knock-off version of a book by Pulitzer-Prize-winning Cormac McCarthy) and wannabe Tenenbaum who dresses in tassels like Jon Voight in *Midnight Cowboy* – the tale of a Texan romantic who comes to New York.

Above: Archaeologist Etheline Tenenbaum (Anjelica Huston) in her office. Each room in the Tenenbaum house teems with idiosyncratic character detail, including Etheline's work on long extinct tribes.

'What is interesting to me is how they deal with the fact that it's all behind them,' said Anderson, revealing a fear that his own youthful gifts might wilt with time and pressure, 'that they must find their self-esteem elsewhere, and that leads them back to their family, where everything begins.'[5]

As producer Scott Rudin (prolific force behind adventurous studio flicks such as *The Truman Show* and *The Addams Family*) pointed out, what 'started out to be more about geniuses, ended up being more about failure.'[6]

Left: Outside the hospital – Royal Tenenbaum (Gene Hackman) and loyal sidekick Pagoda (Kumar Pallana) in the hotel livery of The Lindbergh Palace Hotel … which was a made-up hotel, shot at the real Waldorf-Astoria.

Below: Danny Glover's Henry Sherman makes his feelings known to Huston's Etheline. Perversely, Anderson was inspired to cast Glover as the gentle-natured family accountant thanks to violent performances in *To Sleep with Anger* and *Witness*.

The part of Royal, said Anderson, was written for Hackman 'against his wishes.'[7] Anderson couldn't consciously explain why, but he could see only Hackman as this primal force of a failed father. Hackman had a gravity that made sense. Admittedly, when the actor proved hesitant about taking on this bowling ball of a patriarch – he disliked being 'restricted'[8] to somebody's idea of who he was – both Michael Caine and Gene Wilder were eyed as a replacement. But Anderson wasn't sure he would be able to go through with the movie without Hackman.

That measure of belief in the fit between actor and character was all Anderson really had to offer. 'There was no money,'[9] he admitted. Everyone in his all-star cast was working to scale. It was emblematic of his swift rise to the status of artist that by only his third film, and still only thirty-one, actors saw the credibility on offer by accepting an invitation to Wesworld.

No one could fault Anderson for his determination, and after eighteen months of genteel harassment via phone, email, dozens of letters, further drafts of the screenplay, and a painting of Hackman in character surrounded by the cast, the star was persuaded that he was key to the project.

Life and art blurring at the edges, it proved an uneasy relationship. Put it this way, Gene didn't take to Wes. Having deigned to take the role, he didn't want to be talking things through with this willowy intellectual. Equally, Anderson felt intimidated by Hackman's status as one of America's greatest actors (if the Californian-born, New York-trained icon needs further introduction, you would start with *Bonnie and Clyde*, *The Conversation*, *The Poseidon Adventure*, and Oscars for *The French Connection* and *Unforgiven*). James Caan had required handling on *Bottle Rocket*, but he was there for only three days and

it was easier to temporarily bend the movie around the star; while Bill Murray had been a pussycat on *Rushmore*. Hackman's Royal was the irregular heartbeat of the entire film.

In an attempt to assert his will, Anderson tried a form of reverse psychology, pointedly taking Hackman's co-stars aside to discuss scenes. Curious, Hackman would often follow, before he got wise to the ruse and called his bluff, pulling Anderson aside for a chat. Fittingly, this took place inside the games closet of the Tenenbaum mansion, an Andersonian repository of board-game classics (whose titles warp into metaphors: *Risk, Operation, Hangman, Jeopardy, Go to the Head of the Class*) and established venue for family tête-à-têtes. Hackman immediately started screaming at the young director. How dare he play these games? Who did he think he was? Anderson, to his credit, remained cool.

Above: A de-aged Royal Tenenbaum (Hackman) and favourite child Richie (Amedeo Turturro, son of actor John Turturro) seen in one of numerous flashback montages. Variants on the brown suits each wears can be found across Anderson's movies and in his wardrobe.

Opposite: Hackman and Anderson confer in a moment of calm. The director would find his star less than compliant. Hackman felt he didn't need to discuss scenes, but may also have been channelling the truculent nature of his character.

'Why are you doing this Gene?' he responded.

'Because you're a c**t,' the actor fumed.

'You don't mean that,' said Anderson steadily.

Hackman maintained he did.

'You're going to regret these things you're saying Gene,' replied Anderson. 'You don't believe them.'[10]

He was right. The next day, Hackman skulked on the edge of the set, waiting for his moment. When it came, he apologized to the director for his loss of temper (which Hackman's agent later informed Anderson was hardly unheard of; it was part of his process), but his frustrations never fully departed. Anderson mentioned the 'seething'[11] whenever he attempted to tinker with a scene.

Whatever the gathering of storm clouds behind the scenes, they clearly contributed to the emotional currents within the film. Hackman becomes

Royal to the tips of his shiny shoes, giving the monomaniacal dandy whispers of genuine heart and timing his convivially obnoxious put-downs to perfection. Rarely had Hackman been so slippery: only his puffed-up Lex Luthor in *Superman* (1978) comes close. And the actor was feeding from his own case history.

In a quieter moment, Anderson recalled Hackman talking about how his father had left his family when he was thirteen or so. 'He just described this moment of his father driving down the street, and Hackman and his friends were playing in the street, and his father drove by. And Hackman saw him driving by, and his father kind of waved from the window but didn't stop the car. And it was the last he saw him for ten years. And Hackman had really choked up when he was telling it.'[12]

Royal was rubbing off on Hackman. 'He's coming to terms with his

mortality,'[13] he said, genuinely feeling he wanted to make amends. Royal might have a left a trail of discord, but he is not quite the villain of the piece.

A short word on bad dads: Anderson once worried he might make an awful father given the number of dud pops he has featured in his films. They are a storybook staple, of course. But in Anderson's hands, they are as regular as bad weather, the catalyst of misfortune and hand-me-down neuroses. Big kids, stuck in states of wilful arrested development. An exhibition entitled Bad Dads is held in San Francisco every year, entirely devoted to paintings and sculptures based on Anderson's world, led by lamentable father figures such as Herman Blume (depressed), Royal Tenenbaum (selfish), Steve Zissou (jealous), Mr. Fox (egotistical), and Mr. Bishop (very depressed).

Anderson was quick to report that his father, Melver, was not a bit like

Royal. 'He was always worried that this was my take on him, which is totally wrong, but it's been hard to kind of, you know, convince him that it's not him.'[14]

Whereas Etheline bears a quite deliberate, if not wholly rationalized comparison to Anderson's mother Texas. Calm, loving, and academic (everything Royal is not), she was written with what Anderson saw as Huston's 'warmth and sophistication'[15] in mind, and some unspecified intuition about her famous background being right for the part. As soon as she said yes, Huston received drawings (by Eric Chase Anderson) of the character in small suits and strange hairdos along with photographs of Anderson's mother.

'He even produced his mother's old eyeglasses for the early scenes,' recalled Huston. 'I asked him, "Wes, am I playing your mother?" I think he was astonished by that idea.'[16]

Having so many established stars required an adjustment in how Anderson would 'do his own thing.'[17] He would have to give them space, and leave himself open, as far as possible, to spontaneity. Nevertheless, the script remained sacrosanct and the world around them tightly controlled. You can see where ripples might stir in strong personalities not yet fluent in Anderson's ways.

Pouting, misunderstood, chain-smoking Margot, eyes enshrouded in raven-feathered mascara and inhabited with brittle indifference by Paltrow, is a playwright like Max in *Rushmore*, if more established. Her branch of the Tenenbaum family tree features a particular romantic pile-up, in which Margot, unhappily married to neurologist Raleigh St. Clair (Bill Murray – morose), is having an affair with Eli (Owen Wilson – manic), while her non-blood brother Richie, Eli's best friend (point of fact: once again Luke Wilson is Owen's brother in life but not in

Above: Eldest Tenenbaum offspring Chas (Ben Stiller) with his identikit sons Ari (Grant Rosenmeyer) and Uzi (Jonah Meyerson). Note the symmetrically arranged shot, the Anderson signature that came of age with his family drama.

Opposite above: Margot Tenenbaum (Gwyneth Paltrow) and Etheline (Huston) in matching dresses. Paltrow, for one, had to adjust to the fact Anderson had the entire movie mapped out in his head beforehand, right down to the colour of costumes and brand of cigarettes (Sweet Aftons).

Opposite below: The idea of the headband worn by former tennis champ Richie (Luke Wilson) was to recall famed seventies tennis icon Björn Borg.

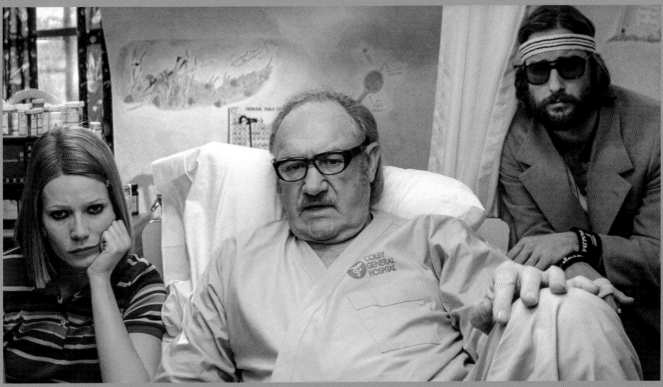

the film), is in love with Margot. A love shared but not reciprocated.

Since his meltdown on the professional tennis circuit, third-child Richie has been avoiding Margot by circumnavigating the world alone by passenger liner. This idiosyncrasy referenced the time Anderson travelled to Europe to promote *Rushmore*. Like Stanley Kubrick, Anderson doesn't like to fly, so he went alone on the *QE2*. He did his US promotional tour for *Rushmore* in a converted school bus. Anyhow, he had a thoroughly miserable time on the *QE2*, surrounded by antique couples. 'You're not supposed to go by yourself on the boat in the first place,'[18] he sighed, spending most of the six-day voyage monitoring the ship's bearing.

Having Stiller as Chas, bitter eldest child and crushed widower neurotically insulating his boys from harm, came about because the comedy star was by now the friend and frequent onscreen partner of

Wilson. Plus, he related. He too had grown up in New York – and, as a sometime director, adored Anderson's vision for a Big Apple of his eye – the son of performers Jerry Stiller and Anne Meara.

Nothing is by chance in the mosaic of Anderson's designs, and each of the three Tenenbaum children is played by an actor from a show-business family. Paltrow's mother is actress Blythe Danner and her father director Bruce Paltrow, and the Wilsons are brothers. Moreover, Huston, as their mother, tots up legendary director John Huston as her father, actor Danny Huston as her brother, Jack Nicholson as a one-time lover, and an entire lifetime in the spotlight.

'It's part of what draws you to them, and makes them seem right for the parts,' mused Anderson. 'It all gets woven in.'[19] They all brought with them matching baggage.

On the flip side, an analogy is often drawn between family and the collective

cast and crew who make a movie – something Anderson really runs with. His films bloom out of intimate productions; stories about families made by a surrogate family of collaborators who return again and again: quirky souls like the Wilson brothers, Murray, Jason Schwartzman, Huston, Willem Dafoe, Saoirse Ronan, and Adrien Brody (though not Hackman). By the next film, *The Life Aquatic with Steve Zissou*, the central, extended, messed up family is a film crew.

Above: Richie (Luke Wilson) and Margot (Gwyneth Paltrow) face up to the recent return of their father. Note the flow of the Anderson palate: the colour scheme of the costumes blends perfectly with the sofa, lampshades, walls and stained glass.

THE ROYAL ANDERSON COMPANY

The key purveyors of the Wes Anderson Method

Bill Murray: *(Rushmore, The Royal Tenenbaums, The Life Aquatic with Steve Zissou, The Darjeeling Limited, Fantastic Mr. Fox, Moonrise Kingdom, The Grand Budapest Hotel, Isle of Dogs, The French Dispatch):* From *Rushmore* onwards, Anderson's lucky star and movie dad, he has appeared in all but one of his films.

Owen Wilson *(Bottle Rocket, The Royal Tenenbaums, The Life Aquatic with Steve Zissou, The Darjeeling Limited, Fantastic Mr. Fox, The Grand Budapest Hotel, The French Dispatch):* Anderson's college friend and first leading man; has been a mainstay of his universe, playing variations on dashing and neurotic, and the dashingly neurotic. He is also the co-writer of the first three Andersons, but didn't appear in *Rushmore*.

Jason Schwartzman *(Rushmore, The Darjeeling Limited, Fantastic Mr. Fox, Moonrise Kingdom, The Grand Budapest Hotel, The French Dispatch):* Part of the Coppola clan, so not exactly an Anderson discovery. Still, his role as Max Fischer in *Rushmore* began not only a fruitful partnership with the director, but a fine acting career. Like Wilson, he also writes.

Anjelica Huston *(The Royal Tenenbaums, The Life Aquatic with Steve Zissou, The Darjeeling Limited, Isle of Dogs):* The original Mother Superior of Anderson's troubled dynasties, Huston is another scion of a famous Hollywood family.

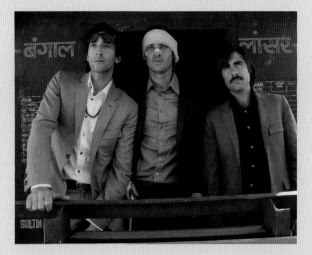

Left: The brothers Whitman from *The Darjeeling Limited*, as played by a trio of Anderson regulars – Adrien Brody, Owen Wilson, and Jason Schwartzman.

Adrien Brody *(The Darjeeling Limited, Fantastic Mr. Fox, The Grand Budapest Hotel, The French Dispatch):* Literally jumped the Anderson train for *The Darjeeling Limited*; another of the thoughtful line of onscreen avatars for the director.

Willem Dafoe *(The Life Aquatic with Steve Zissou, Fantastic Mr. Fox, The Grand Budapest Hotel, The French Dispatch):* Among his assignments, the New York actor has played a huffy German engineer, a jive-talking rat, and a fascist heavy with fangs, so surely counts as the most versatile of Anderson's regulars.

Tilda Swinton *(Moonrise Kingdom, The Grand Budapest Hotel, Isle of Dogs, The French Dispatch):* Special mention for her ancient and horny dowager Madame D. in *The Grand Budapest Hotel*, performed beneath platefuls of prosthetic and a tottering wig.

Kumar Pallana *(Bottle Rocket, Rushmore, The Royal Tenenbaums, The Darjeeling Limited):* Ran Anderson's local coffee shop in Dallas, before launching a second career as an actor thanks to his former customer. Special marks for stabbing Gene Hackman.

Luke Wilson *(Bottle Rocket, Rushmore, The Royal Tenenbaums):* Former flatmate and Wilson brother, he was the romantic face of early Anderson (see also the third Wilson brother, Andrew, who had small roles in those first three Anderson movies).

Edward Norton *(Moonrise Kingdom, The Grand Budapest Hotel, Isle of Dogs):* A latecomer to the family, he has since proved willing to don knee-length shorts in the name of art.

Special mention: Eric Chase Anderson, part-time actor, concept artist, and Anderson's actual brother.

The other great impulse behind *The Royal Tenenbaums* was the desire to tell a New York story. Anderson had recently made his dreamed-of move to Manhattan, escaping glib Los Angeles for the tumble of art, literature and imported films amid the snarled-up traffic and skyscrapers that were straight out of the homegrown movies. An embroidered vision of the city fostered by reading back issues of its illustrious intellectual weekly and bastion of smarty-pants New York mythology *The New Yorker*. It was always in Anderson's mind that the Tenenbaums would live in a big, old house somewhere in a dream Manhattan.

'I'd always had this fascination with New York,' he explained of his architectural thinking. 'I'm from Texas, but there were so many novels and movies that are New York novels and movies that were among my favourites, and so I had this sort of, not quite accurate idea of what New York was like.'[20]

He was going to create a New York of the mind like in *Rushmore's* ersatz *Serpico*. While shot on location from 26 February 2001 for sixty days, his film was assembled from second-hand descriptions in movies, songs, books, photos and paintings. Take your pick: here is the compartmentalized tenement block of Hitchcock's *Rear Window*; the gilt-edged ballrooms of Martin Scorsese's Edith Wharton adaptation *The Age of Innocence*; the lilting Central Park cool of Simon & Garfunkel; and a medley of Andy Warhol art and Robert Frank snapshots. The characters come dressed like *New Yorker* cartoons. The when is equally hard to pin down: it could be the sixties, seventies or eighties, or a blend of all three. This is the nostalgic prehistory of Anderson time.

There is a brief scene of Royal winning over his grandsons by racing go-karts in gleeful homage to the brutal car chase beneath Bensonhurst Elevated Railway in *The French*

Connection, starring a furious Hackman. Apart from the in-joke, this marks another of Anderson's light-footed parodies of hard-knuckle thrillers.

Director Peter Bogdanovich, born and bred in the big city, had recommended a couple of plays for him to check out, marvelling at how Anderson could 'see the whole movie in his head long before he shoots.'[21] He made films like putting on a play, devising elaborate scenery and assembling a company of actors.

Uppermost, Anderson wanted to create his version of the literary New York finessed like cut glass by greats such as F. Scott Fitzgerald, Dawn Powell, and the multi-tome saga of J.D. Salinger's Glass family from Upper Manhattan.

The film is structured inside a borrowed library book, the first edition of *The Royal Tenenbaums*, narrated via voice-over by Alec Baldwin (most successful member of the Baldwin brood). 'I had this idea that rather than the movie being based on a book, the movie would be the book,'[22] said Anderson, firmly establishing his

formula for fixing his stories within a symbolic framework.

A brief study of Anderson's things within things: what began with the suggestion in *Rushmore* that Max's entire life is a theatrical production by having the film open with the parting of plush stage curtains, has developed into a motif. In *The Royal Tenenbaums* we find the film nesting in a book, and the same goes for *Fantastic Mr. Fox*, only that is the actual book by Roald Dahl. In *The Darjeeling Limited* we start in a cab in an Indian city, bombing through traffic in the style of the national cinema. The cab contains Bill Murray in the style of Wes Anderson. In the otherwise dreamy *Moonrise Kingdom* the tale is surrounded by a brusque meteorologist's documentary, as if indeed reporting on the weather. By the time we get to *The Grand Budapest Hotel*, there is a girl reading a book of the same title – then a plunge back in time to the author filming a documentary remembering the man who told him the story that is the film. This is all less wilful eccentricity than a helpful tip on how to engage with the story to follow. In other words, the

Opposite: The brooding brood face Royal amid the fading grandeur of their brownstone. Note the psychological positioning of the three grown-up children: Richie and Margot up close, while Chas hovers in the doorway.

Below: The young Margot (Irina Gorovaia) in front of her carefully categorized library of theatrical greats. All books in Anderson's films confer meaning. To wit: Margot is clutching a copy of Eugene O'Neill's play *The Iceman Cometh* – about a cynic who delivers unvarnished truths much like Royal.

framing mechanism sets a tone, be it theatrical, bookish, regional, scientific or historical.

Anderson was adamant that they use a real house for the fictional Tenenbaum domicile. With the cast working to complicated schedules of availability, he wanted a base; somewhere they could go and claim a room. He was after that underlying sense of gravity in a parental home – the force that pulls stray children back into orbit. The way houses so often anchor movies. 'They wouldn't have that sense of history if they filmed on a soundstage,'[23] he said.

The title springs from Orson Welles's second film *The Magnificent Ambersons*, a 1942 period drama and flawed masterpiece – based on Booth

Tarkington's 1918 novel – that spins its familial web around the Amberson mansion. The magnificent Anderson confirmed this period ensemble to be his chief inspiration, though the name 'Tenenbaum' was borrowed from college friend Brian Tenenbaum, who had a sister named Margot.

Anderson regularly turns to Welles for inspiration. 'He likes the big effect, the very dramatic camera move, the very theatrical device,'[24] he enthused, a chip off the old genius. Welles tends to be larger than life.

The house also gave the film its identity. Given the cascade of montages tracing multiple backstories like flip books, and the numerous strands of story, the script called for 240 scenes

Above: However cramped it might get, Anderson was determined to shoot in an actual house, not on soundstages, so the actors would feel the history of the building.

Opposite: The house was found after an extensive search in Harlem, and as soon as he laid eyes on its Edith Wharton-style exterior, Anderson knew this was the place.

in 250 locations. And Anderson was insistent anything that characterized New York was forbidden. There were to be no clichés, no postcard landmarks for the illiterate viewer. Hackman expressed continued bafflement during a scene in Battery Park on the shores of the Hudson River when co-star Kumar Pallana (in his third Anderson as Royal's devoted if unpredictable man-servant and former assassin Pagoda) was precisely placed in the frame to hide the Statue of Liberty.

Anderson and Wilson invented the Gypsy Cab Company, Green Line buses, whole street references (you will not find the '375th Street Y' on any map), and The Lindbergh Hotel, where Royal lives on credit, using the lobby of the Waldorf.

The house was the centre of the shoot's small universe, a classic storybook New York brownstone found in Harlem, in the Sugar Hill area on 144th Street and Convent Avenue

(another site of pilgrimage among dedicated fans). Anderson had been scouting the area with his friend George Drakoulias when he saw this corner house, its grandeur on the turn like the pile in *The Magnificent Ambersons.* He thought, immediately, 'That's the place.'[25] It was due to be remodelled, but Anderson got the owner to hold off for six months and moved in.

Everything within was retrofitted to his carefully devised blueprint, like the cutaways of mansions he drew as a kid. The specific merger of character, prop and location – and the diorama-like profusion of it all (that doll's-house cliché so readily applied by critics) – reached fruition. Anderson's holistic stamp collection is now a multi-layered puzzle book to be absorbed and decoded at leisure.

From the Tenenbaum flag flying from the turret to Etheline's study stacked with back issues of *National*

Geographic and numbered bits of pottery (Anderson's mother had been consulted), everything in the frame tells a story. The bedrooms belonging to each of her three offspring remain filled with the artefacts of their childhood excellence. In Margot's room can be found a miniature theatre and shelves of alphabetized plays, in Richie's room are his tennis trophies, and in Chas's bustling office are found the 'Dalmatian mice'[26] he bred for his sixth-grade moneymaking scheme. The tiny spotted rodents were created by no greater means than a Sharpie Pen. Anderson became fascinated with this one mouse that would, without fail, run counter-clockwise to the others. 'It was really like autism or something,'[27] he said, reflecting that he tended to use that mouse the most.

Volumes could be devoted to cataloguing every item, colour (top notes: autumnal golds and milkshake pinks), and prearranged tableau to be sampled by that symmetrical framing and those laconic dolly shots, left to right, passing between walls like a ghost.

From Royal's pin-stripe threads to Chas and his boys in matching scarlet Adidas tracksuits to Richie's Björn Borg headband, everyone's costume is exactly that: a costume. Anderson spoke in terms of each character having a 'uniform.'[28] The Tenenbaum children, has-beens at thirty-something, have the same dress and hairstyle as they did when their parents split.

Circulating like air through this snow-globe microverse come misty yesteryear sounds from the Rolling Stones, the Beatles, and Ravel, music often played on set. 'It was very sensual,'[29] noted Paltrow.

Anyone who has accompanied the Tenenbaums in their travails will have witnessed Anderson's filmmaking handwriting becoming more pronounced. The film opens with a meticulous ten-minute prologue accumulating a thumbnail of biography and topography for each perfectly centred family member alongside a cover version of *Hey Jude*. Later, we get a montage of Margot's many romantic indiscretions (complete with age and location) delivered with the crisp efficiency of a drum fill. The film is literally divided into chapters. It's a quality Anderson shares with Quentin Tarantino, though at a very different frequency and with greater concentration on wallpaper: they shape films as if they are novels, where the structure and chronology can be moved around like a tile puzzle.

For critics, *The Royal Tenenbaums* was a confirmation that Anderson was truly his own man. Whatever bland temptations a studio might have offered, he had not succumbed. 'Wes Anderson simply has a unique way of looking at the world,' cheered Tim Merrill in *Film Threat*, 'and through him the ridiculous is made sublime.'[30]

In *Entertainment Weekly*, Lisa Schwarzbaum caught that affection for his characters: 'Anderson never demands love or attention, never demeans, never makes fun of his dollhouse family even when being funny about their extremis.'[31]

The clever-clogs style once again bequeaths a psychological realism. This is a fairy-tale of New York with thorns of genuine hurt and loneliness. The script is as pin-sharp as the suits, razor-edged with caustic wit and softened with a kind of deadpan sincerity. When Royal is exiled from hearth and home for the second time, caught out in his deceptions, he reports to his stony-faced clan that the last six days have been possibly the best of his

life. Then Baldwin's voice-over tunes in again, 'Immediately after making this statement, Royal realized that it was true.'[32] All of Anderson's films are poised on such moments of realization.

There will be a flurry of calamity, failed suicide attempts and genuine funerals before matters draw to a close, but a degree of self-knowledge and contentment will be attained. The same goes for Anderson (and his backers), for *The Royal Tenenbaums* became his first genuine hit: taking $71 million around the world and winning an Oscar nomination for Best Original Screenplay (which felt stingy, at the very least: what of the art direction?)

'The humour I like is humour that comes from people's insecurities and vulnerabilities ... '[33] he said. More than any other film across Anderson's unclassifiable dance between genres, the *Tenenbaums* is a tragedy masquerading as a comedy. Or is it the other way around?

Above: The ties that bind – the Tenenbaum clan including outliers Henry Sherman (Glover) and Pagoda (Pallana) on the right, and doomed beagle Buckley (named after doomed singer Jeff Buckley) in the centre.

Opposite: Anderson hitches a lift with Owen Wilson and Paltrow in the boot of Eli Cash's 1964 cream-coloured convertible Austin-Healey 3000 – another vintage touch.

THE LIFE AQUATIC WITH STEVE ZISSOU

For his fourth film, Wes Anderson unveiled his most ambitious, elaborately designed and divisive yarn to date: a *Boy's-Own* tale of illegitimate sons, man-eating sharks and the existential pangs of a has-been oceanographer

'Murray is different,' began Wes Anderson, pondering what it was about Bill Murray that draws him like an inquisitive moth to a sardonic flame: 'He's the one that I'm most likely to describe as a genius, which I don't necessarily mean as the highest compliment even, just as more a description of him.'[1]

You can't ever predict his thought processes, he explained. The sentences that come out of his mouth are the last thing you expect. Even with the lines you provide him, something in his delivery unearths unforeseen layers and hidden punchlines. Every so often he goes off like a hand grenade.

Following his debut in *Rushmore*, Murray has become the Cheshire Cat of Wes's Wonderland, only with more of a wince than a grin. The actor-comedian-genius embodies the essential weather pattern of all Anderson's films: a comic front preceding a rainstorm of sorrow. 'You can't get around it, really,'[2] mused Anderson: Murray radiates melancholy.

By 2003, fresh off an Oscar nomination for *Lost in Translation*, Sofia Coppola's hit exploration of an actor's middle-aged discontent, it was clear Murray's charming ennui was working for audiences too. His career had been reinvigorated.

Yet only once has Murray been Anderson's star attraction. It's as if such a piquant flavour must be used sparingly for fear of overwhelming the dish. You run the risk of too much Murray. Which with Anderson's fourth film was really the point. More even than with Gene Hackman's blowhard Royal Tenenbaum, this is the tale of a monumental ego all at sea. Washed-up oceanographer Steve

Above: The life erratic – Murray brings all his comic brio and melancholic aura to the titular oceanographer, a character it takes more than one viewing to truly appreciate.

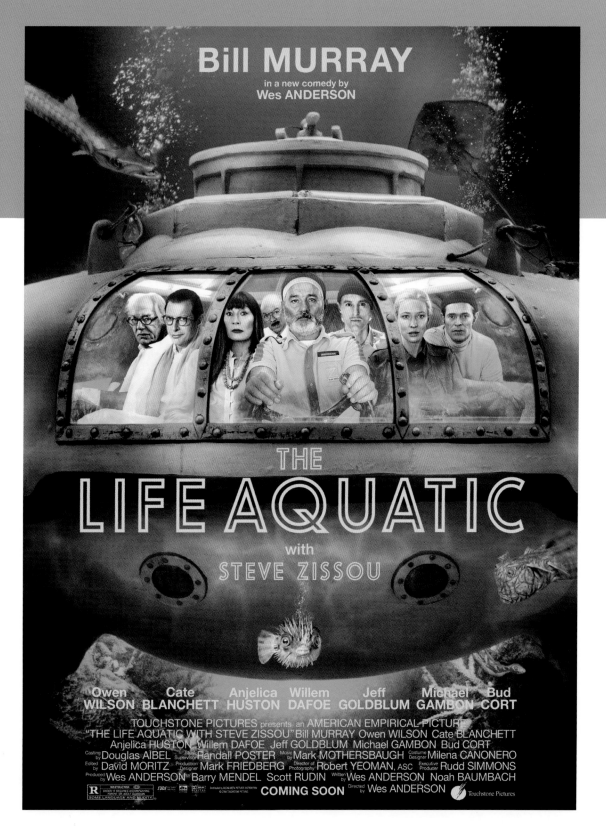

Right: With its ambitions to shoot on the high sea, as well as using elaborate sets and stop-motion special effects, *The Life Aquatic with Steve Zissou* remains the most expensive film Wes Anderson has ever made.

Zissou is looking to revive his glory days, but is also intent on revenge against the fabled jaguar shark that ate his partner. Even for Anderson it was kind of 'out there.'

From the inception of *The Life Aquatic with Steve Zissou* – that namecheck flags up the film's focus on a singular soul – Zissou began to take on Murray's Moon-like face. It was more than casting; somewhere in the writing process they became permanently fused. They are emanations of one another, Murray and Zissou. Anderson knew Murray would be uninhibited, bringing all that comic jazz to the part ... so Zissou had to be charismatic. His crew willingly confront danger for their errant captain – and when considering how to capture this force of personality, Anderson recalled a Sheryl Crow concert he'd attended with Murray in Central Park, and their walk back

afterwards through New York. At each corner they'd gathered more followers, people jaywalking across the traffic the join the throng. By the time they'd reached the parking lot, there must have been forty people trailing in Murray's wake. 'I've never seen anything like it my life,'[3] said Anderson. He would reinvent that memory for the finale of his film. Zissou was 'also tormented, angry and very agitated.'[4] As with everything Murray did, Anderson knew his star would offer wells of darkness beneath the droll surface.

From the star's perspective, it was quite a role. Here was an adventurer-filmmaker, a man of action who has lost direction. The Disney press materials describe him as 'endearingly off-course.'[5] Murray was enthralled by the sheer quantity of detail in the screenplay: dialogue, action, humour, pathos, and real emotion bursting over

the film like waves. The whole piece was awash with metaphors.

'Steve is obviously deeply flawed, a guy driven by his desires, continually blind to people around him, almost infantile in a sense,' he noted proudly. 'But more than that, Steve is someone who doesn't put on a mask to disguise who he is. He simply lets fly.'[6]

Anderson knew that Murray would play all the angles of this larger-than-life personality as honestly as possible. In story terms, it is Zissou's flaws that are appealing, and Murray would wear them like a wetsuit. Anderson was setting his new film in the liminal zone of the star's imperious boredom, more than on the Neapolitan coastline. But Zissou was born long before Anderson ever met Murray.

WES ANDERSON LIMITED

A chronological journey through the career
of America's most distinctive director

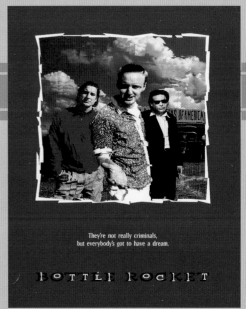

1996

1989
The Ballad of
Reading Milton
(Short Story)
Author

1993
Bottle Rocket (Short)
Director, Writer

1996
Bottle Rocket
Director, Writer

2001

2002
IKEA Unböring campaign
'Kitchen' (Commercial)
Director

IKEA Unböring
campaign 'Living Room'
(Commercial)
Director

2001
The Royal Tenenbaums
Director, Writer, Producer, Voice

2006
American Express 'My Life, My Card'
(Commercial)
Director, Writer, Actor

2007
AT&T 'College Kid', 'Reporter',
'Mom', 'Architect', 'Actor' and
'Businessman' (Commercials)
Director

aNatalie Portman

2007
Hotel Chevalier (Short)
Director, Writer

2009

MATHIEU **AMALRIC**   ISABELLE **HUPPERT**

D'APRÈS LE LIVRE
"FANTASTIQUE MAÎTRE RENARD" DE ROALD DAHL,
L'AUTEUR DE "CHARLIE ET LA CHOCOLATERIE"

UN FILM DE
WES ANDERSON

FANTASTIC
MR. FOX

2008
SoftBank 'Mr Hulot'
(Commercial)
Director

2009
Fantastic Mr. Fox
*Director, Writer,
Producer, Voice*

2005
The Squid and the Whale
Producer

Peter Bogdanovich

2006
They All Laughed 25 Years Later:
Director to Director – A Conversation
with Peter Bogdanovich and
Wes Anderson (Documentary Short)
Interviewer

2007

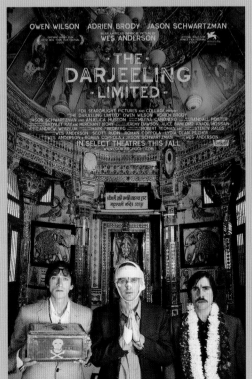

2007
The Darjeeling Limited
*Director, Writer,
Producer*

1998

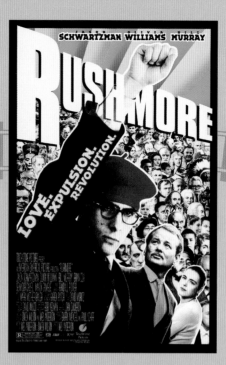

1998
Rushmore
Director, Writer,
Executive Producer

2004

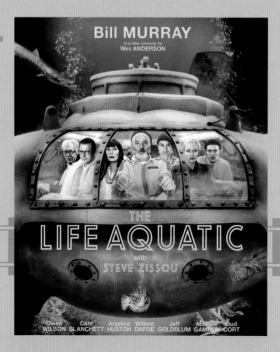

2004
The Life Aquatic With Steve Zissou
Director, Writer, Producer

2015
Bar Luce, Fondazione Prada,
Milan, Italy (Café)
Designer

2016
H&M 'Come Together':
A Fashion Picture in Motion
(Commercial)
Director, Writer

2018

2018
Isle of Dogs
Director, Writer, Producer

2018
Spitzmaus Mummy in a Coffin and
other Treasures: Kunsthistorisches,
Vienna, Austria (Exhibition)
Co-curator (with Juman Malouf)

2014
She's Funny That Way
Executive Producer

2014
The Society of the
Crossed Keys (Book)
Editor, Writer

2014

2014
The Grand Budapest Hotel
Director, Writer, Producer

2012
Sony 'Made of
Imagination'
(Commercial)
Director

2012
Hyundai 'Modern Life'
(Commercial)
Director

Hyundai 'Talk to my Car'
(Commercial)
Director

2012
Prada 'Candy L'Eau' series
(Commercial)
Co-director (with Roman Coppola)

Prada 'Castello Cavalcanti'
(Commercial/Short)
Director, Writer

James Ivory

2010
Conversation with James Ivory
(Documentary Short)
Interviewer

2010
Stella Artois 'Mon Amour'
(Commercial)
Co-director
(with Roman Coppola)

Roman Coppola

2012

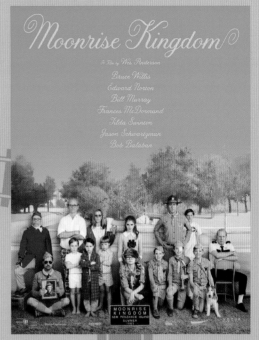

2012
Moonrise Kingdom
Director, Writer,
Producer

2012
Moonrise Kingdom:
Animated Book (Short)
Director (uncredited),
Writer (uncredited)

2012
Cousin Ben Troop
Screening with Jason
Schwartzman (Short)
Director, Writer, Producer

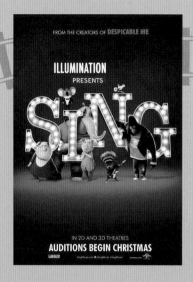

2016
Sing
Voice of Daniel, a giraffe

2017
Escapes (Documentary)
Executive Producer

2020

2020
The French Dispatch
*Director, Writer,
Producer*

When he was a boy, Anderson was obsessed with Jacques Cousteau. The great French oceanographer awoke the world to the splendours of the ocean through a series of Zen documentaries in the fifties and sixties, winning the *Palme d'Or* at Cannes in 1956 with *Le Monde du Silence*. Each one was guided by his famously languid voice-overs. Cousteau, the former naval officer turned conservationist, also co-invented the aqualung and was involved in the development of the underwater camera and water-resistant goggles, and this mix of practicality, wonder and eccentricity charmed Anderson. Cousteau took audiences into the deeps, a world unto itself – full of nature's misfits and oddballs and sunken wrecks.

'I've always loved Cousteau,' confirmed Anderson, who'd made a point of watching *every* one of his documentaries, and reading *all* the books and biographies. 'I love his whole persona.'[7]

Indeed, his love of Cousteau was signalled from the very beginning. Richard Avedon's famous portrait of the diver hangs on the wall of Mr. Henry's place in *Bottle Rocket*, and it is the oceanographer's book that Max pivotally discovers in the library in *Rushmore*: subtle references leading us like breadcrumbs toward Zissou.

In fact, Anderson had wanted to make a movie led by a Cousteau-like character for over fourteen years. It would be about an 'eccentric family at sea,'[8] he said. There exists a short story, not much more than a paragraph, from his college days that describes an oceanographer named Steve Zissou, skipper of the research vessel, the *Belafonte*, with a wife who is really the brains of the operation. Over the intervening years, story and character evolved. Anderson dived deeper into

Above: Keeping a grip on things – the director poses at the wheel of the mini-sub *Deep Search* during a production that would test his ability to maintain control of his ideas.

Zissou's personality – how he had reached a point in his life when 'it all seems to be slipping away.'[9]

From time to time Owen Wilson would ask after the fading oceanographer, but with the actor preoccupied by Hollywood, Anderson turned to Noah Baumbach to help him write the screenplay. Part of a growing New York set, the erstwhile director of realist 'dramedies' (*The Squid and the Whale, The Marriage Story*) would meet him every day at a Manhattan restaurant, where they would sit and make each other laugh until dinner. Looking back, Anderson is often surprised they got anything done.

But a script did emerge, and one with ambitions far beyond anything Anderson had previously attempted. *The Life Aquatic with Steve Zissou* called for boats; sun-kissed, coastal locations; undersea creatures ... and even more exotic humans. The fact that the script came to life in an Italian diner played its part: Italy and its waters became the setting, with the names of dishes borrowed for locations and characters.

Anderson's creative trajectory from Texas to New York was now taking him to the cradle of the European cinema he adored. Unsurprisingly, this would demand a much bigger budget. Persuaded that the success of *The Royal Tenenbaums* meant Anderson's whims had more than cult appeal, Disney stumped up a miraculous $50 million, enabling him to spend four months exploring the depths of Steve Zissou.

Returning producer Barry Mendel saw a director taking wild risks in venturing so far from the 'precise chamber pieces' of *Rushmore* and *The Royal Tenenbaums*. 'He's thrown himself into a chaotic, exterior, fantastical genre film,'[10] he commented.

Which was true, except the film that emerged couldn't feel more archetypally Wes Anderson.

When we meet him, Zissou is verging on despair. He's past his prime and he knows it, though he is putting up a fight. With his devoted but haphazard crew, this 'schlock Jacques Cousteau,'[11] as *New York Magazine* describes him, embarks on a quest (combined with a new documentary) for the mythical jaguar shark which took the life of his great friend and shipmate Esteban (*Rushmore's* Seymour Cassel, beaming away in flashback from beneath a bald cap).

On one level, Anderson and Baumbach had conceived of a modern-day version of *Moby Dick* ... only Herman Melville never had Captain Ahab lounging around in Speedos. Setting forth on his search, thanks to the threadbare funds drummed up by his long-suffering producer (played by Michael Gambon) with typical fatalism, Zissou is certain this is 'the last adventure I've got in me.'[12]

As Murray wisely intuited, it might be Zissou's darkest hour, but the beauty of the character is that he never loses momentum. Zissou keeps going full steam ahead. His life, like Royal Tenenbaum's, has been, until now, unencumbered by introspection. He has a Buster Keaton quality: he's a slapstick hero assailed by the fates, with the indefatigable spirit of the great French silent comedian Jacques Tati.

What makes the seafaring wiles of Steve Zissou so defiantly personal to Anderson is that this is a film about filmmaking. The communal life of the *Belafonte* is a reflection of the community behind the scenes, with many devoted regulars making up his crew. Anderson might even be contemplating the ghost of his own future by focusing on an ageing filmmaker facing up to the fact that his best days are behind him. He had older friends who had reached the point where the muse had withered. The central question that plays on

Zissou's mind is 'Am I ever going to be good again?'[13]

Just as he absorbed bookish New York in *The Royal Tenenbaums*, Anderson would soak up arthouse Italy like blotting paper. Not only was he shooting on and in the sun-blessed waters off the coast of Naples, he was utilizing Rome's legendary Cinecittà Studios, playground

to the mighty Federico Fellini. 'The place is steeped in Fellini still,'[14] he extolled, and there is something of the listless heroes played by Fellini *alter ego* Marcello Mastroianni in Zissou. Before shooting, Anderson also delved into the languorous, elusively plotted masterworks of Michelangelo Antonioni, even using some of the same locations as *L'Avventura*. The air was full of mystery. It was so unlike making an American movie, even Gambon's glasses were modelled on those worn by fabled Italian composer Ennio Morricone.

Tanned by the sunshine, his hair cut boyishly short, the director's handsome appearance took Anjelica Huston by surprise.

Above: Visions in sky-blue – Zissou (Murray) leads out his crew, including financier Oseary (Michael Gambon in a suit), Klaus (Willem Dafoe), Eleanor Zissou (Anjelica Huston), and Vikram (Waris Ahluwalia).

Right: Club Med – Zissou (Murray) and Jane (Blanchett) bask in the sunshine. While the film never commits to a particular setting, Anderson chose the gloriously cinematic Neapolitan coast in Italy.

Below: Murray's Zissou holds court with his faithful crew. As well as Blanchett's Jane, the other non-uniformed character is seventies icon Bud Cort as the bond company inspector Bill Ubell.

Anderson's cast list was growing. After the family-sized ensemble of *The Royal Tenenbaums*, now he had an entire crew. First there was the *Belafonte's* well-salted team of sailors and filmmakers, made up of a mix of new and familiar personae. Like Dignan's mismatched gang in *Bottle Rocket*, the Max Fischer Players staging their war movies in *Rushmore*, and on into the schemes of *Fantastic Mr. Fox*, Zissou is the head of a team.

Huston hardens the dependable sweetness of Etheline Tenenbaum into icy Eleanor Zissou, the brilliant wife and Vice President of The Zissou Society, currently and understandably estranged from her husband. Watching the rapport Huston had with Murray in a single scene in *The Royal Tenenbaums* served as another catalyst in Anderson turning to the story of Zissou next. In *The Darjeeling Limited*, Huston will complete a trio of elusive but phlegmatic mothers, immune to the wounded pride and petty demands of menfolk.

Willem Dafoe makes his Anderson debut as the petulant but adoring engineer Klaus Daimler, unusually prone (for a German and a technician)

to emotional outbursts. Plus, we have Waris Ahluwalia as cameraman Vikram Ray (the name a passing tribute to Indian auteur Satyajit Ray: for more, see *The Darjeeling Limited*), Noah Taylor as physicist Vladimir Wolodarsky (named after family friend, writer and occasional butt of the joke Wally Wolodarsky), and singer Seu Jorge as chilled Brazilian safety expert Pelé, who, in a most Andersonian of touches, serenades the crew with acoustic versions of David Bowie songs in his native Portuguese. Cover versions, Anderson claimed, that Bowie adored.

Two outsiders and dramatic catalysts will arrive in Zissou's genial if scatterbrained kingdom. First, there is heavily pregnant reporter Jane Winslett-Richardson (the name deliberately trailing notes of 'English Rose' actresses), given a jolly-hockey-sticks zeal by the wonderful Cate Blanchett (after both Gwyneth Paltrow and Nicole Kidman dropped out due to scheduling problems).

In what sounds like a scene devised by Anderson, Blanchett fainted during a fitting of the prosthetic stomach and learned she was *genuinely* pregnant.

It was a complete coincidence, she commented, and not some titanic level of method. The producers fretted that the travelling and weather might be too much, but Blanchett, now certain this had all been fated, threw herself in gung-ho. With all her hormonal highs and lows, Jane is as unpredictable as the skipper, although with far better reason. With the off-screen father of her child uninterested, she has been cut adrift. Moreover, her hero, the Great Zissou, whom she has come to profile, is proving somewhat desperate.

Next, he receives the shock news that dapper Air Kentucky co-pilot Ned Plimpton (Wilson, getting a more substantial bite of the cherry once again) is claiming to be his long-lost son. Which automatically files artist-scientist-filmmaker-romantic Zissou within the ranks of Anderson's flawed, cynical, life-hewn father figures. Still, after due consideration, Zissou eagerly embraces the supposition. After all, his new film needs 'a relationship sub-plot.'[15]

As the outsider, Wilson rehearsed his scenes away from the rest of the cast on the roof of the Hotel Eden in Rome,

Left: Jeff Goldblum makes his debut in an Anderson film as rich and slippery oceanographer Alistair Hennessey, a rival to Zissou both in the undersea documentary market and, in one of two love triangles, for the heart of Eleanor (Huston).

where Anderson was based. Together they figured out his Southern accent (borderline absurd, as if he's stumbled out of *Gone with the Wind*), well-bred naiveté, and Errol Flynn moustache. Ned has that natural Wilson jauntiness, but is miles off his hip Hollywood-slacker routine. Anderson wanted this to be a departure for his old friend (maybe even a rescue). Both had been drawn to the 'romantic notion'[16] of explorers as kids, and Anderson decided that Ned would have the same sense of awe about Zissou that he himself had for Norwegian ethnographer Thor Heyerdahl, who once crossed the ocean on a hand-built raft.

Such a stew of familial crisis plots this ocean-going venture firmly in Andersonian waters. Whatever the setting, the surface genre or central species, all his films are really family dramas.

Further proof of a story as emotionally entangled as seaweed, amid the numerous calamities that will befall the possibly final voyage of the *Belafonte* – including but not limited to pirate attacks, intern mutiny, three-legged dogs and death – Zissou and Ned will compete for Jane's affections. Meanwhile, Eleanor has done her worst and taken up with Zissou's arch oceanographic rival Alistair Hennessey, played by Jeff Goldblum, another actor whose particular set of mannerisms are right at home in Anderson's world. Hennessey is another big fan of Zissou.

One other notable new recruit is Bill Udell, the uptight bond company stooge installed onboard to monitor Zissou's spending, who will end up being held hostage by Filipino pirates, shot at, and abandoned, but having the time of his life. Udell is played by diminutive actor Bud Cort who was a Robert Altman regular and star of intergenerational 1971 romantic-comedy *Harold and Maude*, and has therefore had a profound influence on Anderson.

THE WES ANDERSON TOOLBOX

The distinctive shots used to create the 'Anderson touch'

Perfect Symmetry: Basically, the frame is organized so that the most important elements are slap-bang in the middle, with the camera at ninety degrees to the subject. You could run a line horizontally down the centre of the frame and each side would mirror the other.

Filmmakers tend to avoid such formalism because it feels staged (which it is). It also makes editing more apparent. Yet there is something comforting in symmetry. It presents a sense of control over the universe, and allows Anderson to direct our attention to what matters.

It's a style adopted from another of his filmmaking heroes, Japanese master of family dramas Yasujirō Ozu (*Tokyo Story*), who barely moved his camera at all. As they snipe at Anderson, so critics fussed that Ozu was stuck in his ways, producing the same compositions again and again. Ozu was unrepentant. 'I only know how to make tofu,' he said. 'I can make fried tofu, boiled tofu, stuffed tofu. Cutlets and other fancy stuff, that's for other directors.'[33]

What Anderson and Ozu share is the principle that the unbalanced inner world of their characters is made both more pronounced and more poignant when set against pure geometry.

The Long Dolly: Further to Anderson's symmetrical framing, he loves to move his camera – as smoothly as possible – left to right, and occasionally right to left, with the camera restricted to an x/y axis. This is achieved with the camera running along dolly tracks (technically: dolly-tracking shots), doing its utmost to keep pace with the protagonists.

Right: Perfect symmetry – a classic example of Anderson's rectilinear framing from *Isle of Dogs*.

Walls are seldom an impediment. The great 'train of thought' sequence from *The Darjeeling Limited* and Scout Master Ward's inspection of the camp in *Moonrise Kingdom* both spring to mind. This is taken one stage further with the crane shot passing along the interior of the *Belafonte* in *The Life Aquatic with Steve Zissou*, which adds up and down to side to side (see the main text).

Bright Colour Palettes: The colour schemes Anderson choses for his films come pregnant with meaning, but also serve to set a general mood. For example, the woody, autumnal, fox-fur tints of *Fantastic Mr. Fox* or the confectionery-box pinks of *The Grand Budapest Hotel*. Anderson begins each new film sweating over highly specific mood boards (using magazine cut-outs and material swatches) for his production departments. Pastels are common, while entire essays have been written on his use of yellow.

Overhead Shots: Along with side-on shots, Anderson loves to shoot from above as a way of revealing key information. The focus of such shots often comes in the guise of lists, letters, homework, open books, the content of cases, maps, escape plans, record players, control panels, and further Andersonian paraphernalia.

Slow Motion: Muscular action directors like Michael Bay use 'slo-mo' to bask in the evident cool of their explosive sequences, whereas Anderson shifts into slow motion (with the caress of a carefully chosen song on the soundtrack) within a shot to achieve a form of emotional piquancy. Think of the vision of Margot descending from the bus in *The Royal Tenenbaums*, or Max taking his applause following his production of *Serpico* in *Rushmore*, or the Whitman brothers tossing away their baggage at the end of *The Darjeeling Limited*.

Above: The crew of the *Belafonte* are, in many ways, simply another messed-up Anderson family, with old hand Klaus (Willem Dafoe) jealously put out when new recruit Ned (Wilson) moves in on the affections of skipper Zissou.

Above: Documenting
the documentarian –
Blanchett's reporter
fishes for soundbites from
the self-aggrandizing
Zissou (Murray) before
his next dive.

Where formerly it had been a school and a New York brownstone, the closed world of the film was now a boat, the magnificent if rusting *Belafonte*. And the boat itself played a role that – like the other parts – needed to be cast. Anderson was very specific about the type of vessel he had in mind: Second World War vintage, a minesweeper, about fifty metres long. In other words, as close as they could get to Cousteau's converted minesweeper *Calypso* (the *Belafonte*, of course, is named after crooner Harry Belafonte, who sang calypso). The specifications were met by an old minesweeper discovered in Cape Town, and just about sufficiently shipshape to make the long voyage to Rome. There, it was repainted (in white and cobalt blue), and outfitted with an observation deck and towers for exterior scenes. A second vessel was mined for parts.

When they arrived in Italy in September 2003, Anderson arranged a day trip on the *Belafonte* – allowing the cast to bond and hopefully get their sea legs, while maybe enabling him to shoot some footage for the Zissou documentaries we glimpse. They set out for the small volcanic island of Ponza and immediately hit rough seas. Nearly everyone onboard was seasick, but somehow they had a grand time. Being on a boat is very intimate, and Anderson noticed how the cast became strangely loyal to the *Belafonte*.

The vessel's interior had to parallel where Zissou was in his life: it was jerry-rigged, ramshackle, kind of pieced together, with a storybook charm and trained albino dolphins. Another motivation behind the film was the director's desire to build a giant doll's-house cross-section of the ship's interiors, where, in a 'hall-of-fame' sequence, he could unveil Zissou's inner workings by moving a crane shot from room to room – taking in lounge, sauna, lab, kitchen, library, cutting room, engine room, and observation bubble. Anderson referred to it as his 'ant colony,'[17] featuring his actors milling about in this three-storey bisected set built on the Fellini Stage of Cinecittà. Locals would come and marvel.

Contrasting with the rapturous exteriors, the line between fact and fiction becomes thin as the camera pulls back to the verge of revealing it is nothing but fakery. Anderson is testing the lengths to which the audience are willing to believe. Like Max Fischer's scenery, these model-kit sets will become a celebrated feature of his work, as if proving Orson Welles's famous adage that filmmaking is the 'biggest electric train set any boy ever had.'[18] (Anderson's next film would, indeed, be set on a train.) Even Zissou's trained dolphins were feigned with animatronic puppets.

To add to the sensation that this was partly a test run before Anderson's

Left: While shooting on the ocean proved a logistical nightmare, the results are among the most gorgeously naturalistic shots in all of Anderson's films.

Below: Such naturalism was counterbalanced by the extraordinary set built to depict the *Belafonte* at the Cinecittà Studios in Rome. This giant cutaway of Zissou's ramshackle ship gleefully draws attention to itself as a human-sized doll's house.

AQUA MASTER   STATUS

TEMPERATURE   301 K

pH   8.1

commitment to an entirely scale-model stop-motion movie (something that was on his mind), the undersea world is brought to life using the same frame-by-frame exactitude as childhood favourites like *King Kong* and the Ray Harryhausen's *Sinbad* pictures. Visionary animator Henry Selick (who had, in fact, directed Tim Burton's *The Nightmare Before Christmas*) was hired to mastermind sea-life, with Anderson's beady approval.

'I wanted that handmade look to the film,'[19] said Anderson, espousing an essential philosophy. Anything high-tech would somehow spoil the effect. This was a movie about a world-renowned oceanographer – with fake fish. As Anderson and Baumbach were

writing, they would dream up creatures the team would encounter, elaborating on real life. 'We might start with just a stingray,' said Anderson, 'but then we would say, how about a stingray with constellations on it that are glowing – and it developed from there.'[20]

Coloured with what looks like crayon (point in case: the two-inch Crayon Pony Fish), these are the endearingly preposterous, clay-like fauna of an aquatic Wonderland. We are never once fooled into believing they are the living things, but they have an enchanting quality – the fairy-tale figments of Zissou's exotic dreams; the wonder that has gone missing from the rest of his life. 'It was about trying to make something imaginary,'[21] explained

Above: To create his imaginary sea-life, Anderson opted to try stop-motion animation for the first time. Ironically, he wanted his sea creatures to feel fantastical rather than real.

Opposite above: Even if his fish were fakes, Anderson did shoot underwater. He was in luck, as Murray was already an accomplished scuba diver.

Anderson. The mythical jaguar shark, their Moby Dick, kept growing larger and larger: it would end up weighing 150 pounds and measuring eight feet long – possibly the largest stop-motion puppet ever made.

The ocean becomes the equivalent of amniotic fluid inside Jane. When it came to the *Deep Search* – the bubble-shaped submersible (as canary-yellow as the Beatles' Yellow Submarine) that finally ports the crew into the depths – a mini-sub was made from fibreglass and steel with working propellers ... but got no further than a soundstage. Anderson crammed his entire cast (bar Wilson's Ned, who perishes in a helicopter crash – just as Cousteau's son died in a seaplane accident) inside that tiny

yellow egg and bolted them in, which really set the mood.

An interlude on era: from *Bottle Rocket* onwards, the 'when' of Anderson's films has proved as slippery as their genre. Even the evidentially period shenanigans of *The Grand Budapest Hotel* tumble back through multiple generations to land on an undefined ledge somewhen between the wars. 'When' it comes to *The Life Aquatic with Steve Zissou*, the equipment is half rickety and half slick, the overall tenor suggesting Cousteau's fifties-sixties-seventies – but there are state-of-the-art doodads and sonars on Hennessey's vessel. It's all entirely deliberate, though Anderson struggles to explain why he applies this temporal ambiguity. 'It's just

by chance,' he offered hesitantly (for you suspect nothing is by chance in his creative process), 'because I'm drawn to old analogue gear, which sets any movie into a *Blue Velvet*-type unknown period. I like that feeling of displacement.'[22]

There is, in Anderson's films, an attempt to preserve the past. He uses antique techniques, and outmoded technologies and materials, as if even his shoots refuse to be tied to the present. 'We filmed part of the film with old Ektachrome reversal stock,'[23] he explained of the grainy, high-contrast look used for Zissou's campy documentary footage. He loved how it cast 'some weird nostalgic look.'[24] Before filming began, Anderson and his producer Mendel watched endless nature

documentaries, less for the wildlife than to study the shots, and figure out which tools were used to obtain them. There is more handheld camerawork in *The Life Aquatic with Steve Zissou* than in any other Anderson film.

Team Zissou's matching sky-blue sweaters and pants, care of Oscar-winning designer Milena Canonero (*Out of Africa*), were the result of Anderson's directive to have them resemble the crew of a sci-fi show from 1968. The tops were made from the same polyester used in the original *Star Trek*. When Wilson walked out of the fitting looking like a boiled sweet, Anderson's laughing fit sealed the deal. The range ran to winter wear, wetsuits, Speedos and 'Zissou'-inscribed trainers developed by Adidas. The red beanies are a tribute to the one sported by Cousteau, but also chimed with Max's beret in *Rushmore*.

When the action rouses itself to madcap rescues, shoot-outs (with crew-issue Glocks), and downed choppers, you suspect this is what would happen if Anderson were ever chosen to make a Bond film. For all the pinging gunfire, and the camera careening along dolly tracks to keep up, the action scenes feel like another lark. These guys are only play-acting at being mainstream.

During an on-stage Q&A with *New York Times* writer David Carr, Anderson confessed quite seriously (or as near as we can tell) that he had an idea for his own entry into the 007 canon, entitled *Mission Deferred*. 'My idea is that the Cold War is over and there's no gig,' he said, unable to keep the intrigue out of his voice. The gadgets included a 'great coffee machine.'[25]

He added that he has never had to fend off the regular Hollywood offers. Still, you could see a fit with something already as whimsical as a *Harry Potter* or a Dickensian tale.

The elements played havoc with Anderson's mania for control. Any director of high-sea escapades would tell him that the ocean is the most uncooperative of cast members. Setting up shots was agonizing, and frequently involved lining up a flotilla of boats only to find the sun had gone. There was a relief in having to quell his own perfections – but it was as tough as things had got so far in his career … even harder than negotiating the turbulent waters of Gene Hackman.

Murray laid it on thick in interviews. How exhausting it all was. How he'd had to spend months away from his family. But that only fed into Zissou's slump. 'I was like this lonely sailor at sea,' he noted, 'and it fit with the mood of the story.'[26] Anderson waved it away: this was just Bill playing to the cameras. 'It wasn't like *Lawrence of Arabia* or anything.'[27]

The *Life Aquatic with Steve Zissou* is classified as the grand Anderson folly. Fans filled the stalls, but this was a big, expensive, multifaceted film that stayed niche in its appeal. A worldwide gross of $38 million did not impress Disney – it remains Anderson's biggest flop. Critics hummed and hawed where once they had purred. At fifty-six percent on *Rotten Tomatoes*, the review aggregator site, it is statistically the worst-reviewed of all his films. What once had been brilliant eccentricity was seen as meandering toward the purely annoying. Anderson was dangerously close to 'over-calculated, under-fed whimsy,'[28] reported Anthony Quinn in the *Independent*; he also lamented the lack of a decent sparring partner to earn Murray's magnificent scorn. It was undoubtedly clever, but felt like some 'secret and melancholy game'[29] that we weren't privy to, pouted Anthony Lane in the *New Yorker*.

Questions were asked in film circles. Could there be such a thing as too much Anderson for its own good? Strangely, to some extent Anderson thought he was trying to broaden his appeal. Walking the line of what is corny and what moves him, it's a subtle game, this silly-seriousness. As Ryan Reed said in his ten-year retrospective, part of a growing revival, '*Aquatic's* free-flowing eccentricity is anchored by the emotional realism of its cast.'[30]

The genius of Anderson is how he outwits kitsch – something he achieves by leaning into pathos. If everyone is a ball of insecurity, a symphonic quality of human absurdity is achieved, with Murray as conductor. For best results, *The Life Aquatic with Steve Zissou* should be taken as another study in crestfallen spirits. And there is something cathartic in the final plunge of the submersible to confront the eerie beauty of the jaguar shark, the chords of Sigur Rós's *Starálfur* swelling in the background. 'I wonder

if it remembers me,'[31] says Zissou, his guard finally down.

'I feel like there's something about the sea,' said Anderson, caught in a rare moment of self-reflection, 'there are these characters who die, and there's this whole mission that Bill and his gang are on. It's some kind of family they're trying to become. And there's some ocean metaphor, this thing that they're all missing that they want to connect with.'[32]

We're all at sea.

Above: Skippers Murray and Anderson confer. *The Life Aquatic with Steve Zissou* would be the director's most self-reflexive work. It is a film about a filmmaker and his crew.

THE DARJEELING LIMITED

For his fifth film, Wes Anderson ventured even further afield, with the story of three estranged brothers seeking connection in exotic India. It is Anderson's road movie, only on a train...

Whenever posed that wearisome question about where his ideas come from, Wes Anderson quotes the Czech-born English playwright Tom Stoppard. There is never one idea, claimed Stoppard; no single seed from which a tree grows. Various things on his mind simply begin to intersect with one another. The rest is alchemy. 'It's never about one thing in particular,'[1] agreed Anderson. There are at least two. In the case of *The Darjeeling Limited*, it was three.

The first ingredient was brotherly love, or the lack of it. 'I always wanted to do a film about three brothers because I am one of three brothers,' he said. 'We grew up fighting and yet they are the closest people in the world to me.'[2] Which puts the inception point of *The Darjeeling Limited* on the day his younger brother Eric Chase was born in 1972, though the plot took shape in the interim period before *The Life Aquatic with Steve Zissou* in 2003.

Anderson conceived of a trio of distinct brothers, the Whitmans, who had become estranged after the death of their father, and their calamitous, funny, and moving attempts at reconciliation. Which would take place on a train trip, his second ingredient.

After messing about in boats, Anderson was embracing another (hopefully more manageable) vehicular cinematic tradition. A rich history of movies on or about trains dates back to

the Lumière brothers' *The Arrival of a Train*, whose first audiences in 1896 fled in terror from its oncoming locomotive. The list is lengthy: the likes of *Murder on the Orient Express*, *A Hard Day's Night*, *Dumbo*, *Night Train to Munich*, and *Doctor Zhivago* all derive drama from the concept of a location on wheels. 'It moves forward as the story goes forward,'[3] Anderson enthused; there are inherent metaphors in tracks, junctions, and potential derailings for the workings of narrative. Alfred Hitchcock loved trains: *The Lady Vanishes*, *The 39 Steps*, *Strangers on a Train* and *North by Northwest* all took pivotal turns between stations.

Above: Frightening conductor – Waris Ahluwalia returns as the train's chief steward, who is less than impressed by the antics of a trio of American brothers.

Opposite: While entirely fictional, *The Darjeeling Limited* would draw directly on the experiences of the three writers – Anderson, Roman Coppola and Jason Schwartzman – travelling around India on a research trip.

Left: *The Darjeeling Limited* joins the ranks of great cinematic love affairs with trains – alongside Sidney Lumet's adaptation of *Murder on the Orient Express*, shown here with a host of stars, and Albert Finney as Hercule Poirot.

Opposite below: Life and art in merry accord, this behind-the-scenes shot of three stars (Wilson, Brody, Schwartzman) as three Whitmans (Francis, Peter, Jack) hints at how deeply embedded the movie was in its Indian locations.

Anderson, naturally, would devise his own inimitable itinerary. His titular train line would carry the petulant Whitman brothers through northern India, the final ingredient for his new film.

When he was eight years old and growing up in Texas, Anderson's best friend came from India: Madras, to be exact. He provided the first exposure Anderson had ever had to the country, and remembered stories that were 'so alien'[4] to him. As with the literary landscape of New York and the underwater realms of Jacques Cousteau, a quixotic illusion of far-flung India became tethered to his imagination.

While at university, Anderson fell deeply in love with Bengali master Satyajit Ray's lyrical, bittersweet depictions of Indian life (in films such as *Pather Panchali* and the *Apu* trilogy). 'It was also part of my inspiration to want to make movies,'[5] he recalled. What Ray revealed was not the teeming hive of contemporary India, caught between the push and pull of industry and poverty, but a more deep-rooted, cultural vision of a country with ancient bones.

Many moons later, the soundtrack to *The Darjeeling Limited* would feature a collage of samples from the musical scores for Ray's films – and from those of early Merchant Ivory movies, made when they too were enamoured by the subcontinent.

The deciding factor was Jean Renoir's *The River*, a restoration of which was screened to him personally by Martin Scorsese in New York. Set on the banks of the Ganges, this coming-of-age story brought an outsider's eye to the mysterious country, leaving a powerful impression on a young Texan director always looking to the horizon. Stepping out of the screening room onto Park Avenue, he could think of nothing but India. Here, he knew, was where his train 'ought to be.'[6]

Like the New York and Mediterranean (and to an extent the nostalgic Texas) of his previous films, Anderson would conjure up a romanticized India, but this time the clamour of reality refused to be silenced.

To mirror the three Whitmans, Anderson assembled a trio of collaborators over his usual duo, and

together they embarked on a form of living screenwriting. Anderson and surrogate brothers Roman Coppola and Jason Schwartzman (who are real-life cousins) would make their own pilgrimage by rail through India, sampling its delights and deliriums, feeding the trials the Whitmans will face with the raw material of personal experience. Which, when you think about it, is the fullest expression of the Anderson formula – life spun into art.

They discovered a nation that lived up to its fictional promise. 'I fell in love with the place,'[7] sang Anderson. Four weeks were spent fathoming timetables that might as well have been in Sanskrit, as they explored a country that mixed urban sprawl with great expanses of desert and mountains like a David Lean movie. None of them had been so far away from home for so long, and if they didn't achieve spiritual enlightenment, it was life-changing. 'We always said say yes to everything,'[8] said Schwartzman.

The writing had begun in Paris. Anderson had recently bought an apartment there, the next staging post in his literary nomadism, and all three happened to be in the city at the same time. Coppola and Schwartzman were working on sister-stroke-cousin Sofia Coppola's *Marie Antoinette* (whose postmodern design schemes lent toward the Andersonesque).

Anderson presented his fellow writers with an opening scene, where the middle one of the three brothers dashes to leap aboard a departing train, while an American businessman is left defeated on the platform (we'll come back to this), but he had no idea what would happen next. They would alternate between Anderson's apartment and local cafés. Separate venues were designated for different discussions. One was for technical matters: who they would hire, how many days they needed, the nuts and bolts of the shoot. The other was purely for storytelling, and the preparation of a rough draft to be ready for their first-hand baptism in the real thing.

Once in India, they worked by throwing ideas around, telling stories, making each other laugh, taking notes, before finally turning to the portable typewriter. Anderson served as stenographer.

'Our train journey ended up being us sort of acting out what we'd written as much as it was us writing,'[9] he laughed, but the point was that virtually everything they experienced found its way into the story. When their portable printer blew up – it was something to do with adaptors – the calamity was fed into the screenplay in the form of a reluctant laminating machine.

They built up backstories for the brothers, with each of the three writers contributing to each character. These were details that might never appear in the film, but widened the bandwidth of the Whitmans – a life behind each disappointed face.

The last thing the three amigos did before leaving India was to re-watch Renoir's *The River* in Delhi. A year later, they would all be back to tell the story of the Whitman brothers in earnest. Schwartzman was set to star as the youngest Whitman, Jack, while Coppola would serve as producer and second-unit director.

The three Whitmans were each written with a specific actor in mind, and one of the film's triumphs is how quickly we accept they are related. This is down to three perceptive performances, subtly linked by costume (they all wear suits in different shades of grey, and have matching baggage – we'll come back to this). They might express themselves very differently, but the Whitmans are united in grief, self-absorption and filial antipathy. In comic terms they are like a manically depressed Three Stooges.

Regular Owen Wilson is the oldest Whitman, Francis. In classic Anderson fashion, each brother would arrive broken in an individual way. In Francis' case, the breakage is literal. Throughout their Indian odyssey, his head remains enveloped, like a badly wrapped turban, in bandages from a recent, near-death motorcycle accident (what we later learn was a suicide attempt; to audiences, this seemed to portend Wilson's own widely publicized suicide attempt in August 2007). Francis also walks with a limp, which Wilson facilitated by keeping half a lime in his shoe at all times.

It is the fastidious, wealthy Francis who has devised this attempted reconciliation on foreign soil. Irking his brothers, he has laid out a minute-by-minute itinerary on laminated cards in a form of enforced epiphany (there is a touch of Anderson in his manic demand for control of the story). The film is, among many things, a satire of the cliché of the Westerner seeking transcendence in exotic locations. Whatever Francis has on his menu of spiritual nourishment, the fates and the director have other ideas. Finally ejected from the train (it is purchasing and losing a baby cobra that breaks the camel's back), with nothing but eleven suitcases and a laminating machine, it is the unexpected that will bring them together.

Anderson had never met the New York native Adrien Brody. Nevertheless, he was set on him for Peter, the middle brother. Crookedly handsome, rather like Wilson (about the only asymmetrical thing in Anderson's films are faces), Brody's reputation had soared with an Oscar for Holocaust drama *The Pianist*, but with typical specificity it was his performance as a gutsy depression-era kid in *King of the Hill* that had spoken to Anderson. Luckily, it turned out Brody was a big fan and eagerly leapt onto the moving train. Peter is twitching with anxiety about impending fatherhood (he's a premature bad dad). He had expected to be divorced by now. To the agitation of his brothers, his extensive baggage includes various items (sunglasses, car keys, razor) commandeered from their father's belongings.

Unsurprisingly, Anderson felt the closest affinity with Schwartzman's Jack, the writer-romantic. 'I also relate to his idea that he's going to document what's happening in his life and make it into fiction,'[10] he said. Much to his brothers' aggravation, Jack's stories bear an uncanny resemblance to all their lives.

The fact he goes barefoot immediately recalls the Beatles gadding about in India in search of divine inspiration. The reference 'wasn't so much planned,'[11] said Anderson, but having noticed how much Schwartzman resembled a Beatle with his droopy moustache and mop-top hair, it made sense. More importantly, Jack arrives in India fleeing a yo-yo relationship.

Right: The three Whitman brothers are on a journey less about finding themselves than finding each other. Note the contrast between their grey American suits and the eye-popping Indian orange of the carriage.

A short aside about *Hotel Chevalier*: beside the *Darjeeling* screenplay, Anderson had been writing a short film. Which at first had nothing to do with the Whitmans' misadventures. Entitled *Hotel Chevalier*, it took place in a Parisian hotel room, an explosion of yellow, in which an estranged couple have a pained rendezvous at the sunset of a long, unbalanced relationship.

As he wrote, the films merged. The lead character of *Hotel Chevalier* became Jack, and this poignant episode evolved into a prologue to *The Darjeeling Limited*. 'They were companion pieces,'[12] Anderson realized, a short story compared to the novel. They were still only halfway through the main script when he shot it, with Schwartzman alongside Natalie Portman as his unnamed girlfriend-stroke-ex. Anderson contemplated affixing *Hotel Chevalier* to the front of the movie, before deciding it was more effective to throw us headlong into the blaze of India.

Hotel Chevalier was released separately; a separate compartment, as it were. There is no pressing reason to have seen it before the main attraction ... beyond the insight it offers into Jack's unhappiness, and the credence it gives to the hint that *The Darjeeling Limited* is the film of the story that Jack has written out of his experiences in India – another Russian-doll narrative. *Hotel Chevalier* is the story Jack gets his brothers to read on the train.

India will gradually force its way into the closed-off world of these three narcissistic brothers, each compartmentalized in their own worlds. 'And it takes a lot for them to really open their eyes,' noted Anderson, 'because they're fixated on their own problems.'[13] Slowly, they begin picking up little mementos and stuffing them into their suitcases. Which is exactly what was going on behind the camera as well.

'We did not control it,' said Anderson. 'India became the subject matter.'[14]

Above: Natalie Portman as Jack's tricky ex-girlfriend in a shot that links the film to *Hotel Chevalier*, the separate short that serves as a prologue to *The Darjeeling Limited*.

WES-EN-SCÈNE

Examples of the great refinement, meaning, scope, confection, content and personal touch of the Wes Anderson set

The Art Nouveau of the Grand Budapest Hotel *(The Grand Budapest Hotel):* Constructed in a former department store in Görlitz, Germany, the interior of this impeccable establishment comes with a delicious apple-red lacquer and polished brass fittings. Outside (a model) it looks like a giant cake with a powder-pink façade. Patisserie would be a motif.

The Belly of the Belafonte *(The Life Aquatic with Steve Zissou):* Built as one gigantic set on a soundstage, the labyrinthine, oceanographic below-decks kingdom is injected with a groovy if dated seventies veneer, much like the skipper.

The Sleeper Carriage of the Darjeeling *(The Darjeeling Limited):* The pivotal train is a mix of spice-colour-coded Andersonian whimsy, folksy Indian wonder, vivid prints, and cramped comic possibility.

The Tenenbaum Residence *(The Royal Tenenbaums):* This fraying New York brownstone presents an eclectic yet interlinked mix of designs to match its potpourri of occupants. Thus, for instance, we get the antiques and artefacts of Etheline's busy office compared to the literary boudoir of Margot, with its shelves of categorized plays and zebra-print wallpaper.

Mr. Badger's Office *(Fantastic Mr. Fox):* One of the film's multitude of intricately decorated miniature sets, Mr. Badger's law firm office (offices are a recurrent setting) reveals a harmonious amalgam of Dahl's anthropomorphized fiction and Anderson's time-out-of-loop authenticity. So not only is there a chunky yellow seventies telephone,

antique 'Dicta-Sonic', Post-its and in-tray, but an Apple Mac Pro to match the one in Anderson's Paris apartment.

'Nam *(Rushmore):* It's a feature of Anderson's world building that he builds miniature worlds within those worlds, often in the shape of plays staged within the plot. We view a fulsome amateur production of Benjamin Britten's *Noye's Fludde* in *Moonrise Kingdom*, an early production of one of Margot's plays in *The Royal Tenenbaums*, and most memorably the intricate stage productions put on by Max Fischer in *Rushmore*: including his Vietnam play, *Heaven and Hell*, with replica jet fighter and flamethrower; and his *Serpico* stage-play with a model El Train. Speaking of which, in *Fantastic Mr. Fox* there is a miniature model train and a miniature train.

Suzy's Books *(Moonrise Kingdom):* As an example of the specificity of props, for a trek into the wilderness, smitten runaway Suzy Bishop grabs all the necessities she can think of, including a case full of stolen library

books. Anderson, a bibliophile, would be in complete agreement. Throughout his films, books (mostly made-up titles) play a revelatory role. Suzy's chosen reading matter is of a fantasy orientation, including *Disappearance of the Sixth Grade*, *The Light of Seven Matchsticks*, and *The Girl from Jupiter* (by Isaac Clarke – the name inspired by science fiction venerables Isaac Asimov and Arthur C. Clarke). Anderson and screenwriter Roman Coppola actually wrote passages of fictional fiction for Suzy to read aloud.

Trash Island *(Isle of Dogs):* Divided into zones, not unlike a video game, this abandoned (model) Japanese island, with its pack of abandoned dogs, is a mesmeric example of the multifaceted homaging that goes within Anderson's films. Heaped with rusty debris, the design conjoins the horizontal landscapes of 19th-century Japanese master Hiroshige, *Godzilla* movies, anime, Andrei Tarkovsky's Russian epic *Stalker*, and James Bond movie *You Only Live Twice* (written by Roald Dahl).

Left: The interior of the titular *Grand Budapest Hotel* reveals the gorgeous marriage between set and storyline in the Anderson universe.

Left: Organized chaos – Wilson's Francis (bandaged) is the chief instigator of the trip, which he has packaged as an enforced epiphany. However, fate and India itself will have other ideas.

Opposite: Marc Jacobs designed the Whitmans' symbolic luggage specifically for the film – the initials 'J.L.W.', we come to realize, are those of their recently deceased father. They are literally carrying their father's baggage.

Below: Snake dance – the Whitmans discover that their recently purchased baby python is no longer in its box; one of multiple animal references in the story.

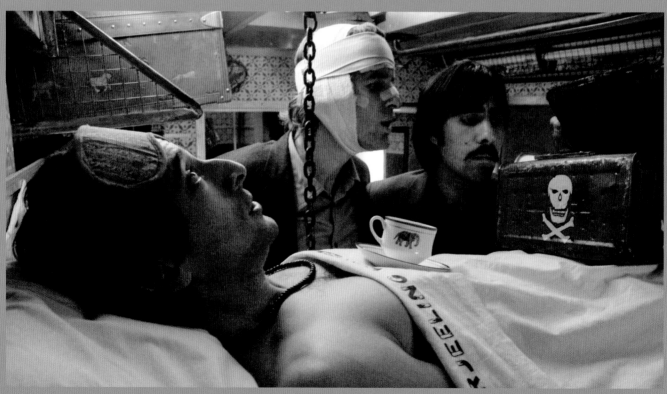

From 15 January 2007, they shot for four months in the desert region of Rajasthan, a near-mythical landscape of northwest India punctuated with dream palaces that looked like miniatures built for the occasion. Anderson thrilled to a 'world filled with colours like nowhere else.'[15] *The Darjeeling Limited*, their fictitious train, travelled along available tracks that ran from Jodhpur to Jaisalmer, near the Pakistani border.

Anderson was determined that the caprices of shooting on location would never become a battle. He strove for a balance between the crisp choreography and pregnant design that had so far defined his work (which is more or less what we get on the train) and an openness toward the spontaneity and mayhem of India (spilling into the frame whenever the brothers leave the carriages).

Compared to the excesses of *The Life Aquatic with Steve Zissou*, the budget was a far more economical $17.5 million. Significantly, Anderson had switched studios to Fox Searchlight. Given this was the arty division of 20th Century Fox, Hollywood had clearly accepted the fact that Anderson wasn't ever going to be a mainstream proposition.

Schwartzman noticed how assured Anderson had become as a director. He could 'just roll with it.'[16] At times, Anderson would find himself actually herding sheep, or goats, while dressed in a linen suit like some stray colonial caught out of the club.

Normally, for any movie set on a train, a set would be built. Something you would doubly expect of Anderson, given how elaborately he assembles his shots. Surely he would concoct an elaborate train set (as it were) which he could open up like a shoebox as

he did with the good ship *Belafonte*. Swayed by his recent travels, he insisted on the opposite. He was intent on using an 'actual'[17] train. No one in his production department could talk him out of it.

After intense negotiation, their request for the use of ten coaches and an engine for three months was granted by Northwestern Railways. It served as Anderson's studio-on-rails, the exterior painted in a vivid mix of cobalt and sky-blue (matching the *Belafonte*), which popped magnificently against the arid backdrop. Meanwhile, the interiors were stripped down and refitted.

On his second Anderson jaunt, and attuned to his director's predilections, production designer Mark Friedberg drew inspiration not only from Indian trains, but luxury lines from all over the world – including the legendary Orient Express. The interior would

be a world unto itself: elaborately Art Deco, mixed with local fabrics and prints. Friedberg then hired Indian artists who covered the walls in a parade of hand-painted elephants.

But there was barely room to swing a camera. How was cinematographer Robert Yeoman going to articulate the emotional reserve and metronomic precision of Anderson's camera moves? Where do you put the lights? If you rigged anything, the actors couldn't move. Putting anything on the roof or more than three feet out from the side of the train was forbidden because of telephone poles.

What was required was ingenuity. They built lighting into the walls of the train. The brothers' sleeper compartment had sliding walls and a track built down the ceiling that made it possible to do dolly shots. Two versions were built, one for each side of the carriage.

Every day was a new adventure. They were working along some of the busiest railway lines in the world, and detours would be announced with little notice. They had to figure out a system for what happened if the train stopped or unexpectedly changed direction. That unpredictability fed into the film. They regularly lost power, leaving them to rehearse scenes in the dark ... something that Anderson found oddly calming.

Outside of the train, the film would feel more 'organic'[18] – a throwback to *Bottle Rocket*, roving the streets of Dallas. Anderson found himself working to the reverse of his natural impulse – where he'd picture how something would look, and ... lo and behold ... it would be created. India fed his imagination – a deluge of strangeness and beauty and humour.

In the tragic but transformative sequence in which the brothers

fail to save one of three boys from drowning, the local villagers were just that – real villagers requisitioned as extras. Anderson still shot with complex framing and long dollies, but there was now what he called a 'merging'[19] of found images with his choreography: east and west not so much colliding as awkwardly embracing.

It emerges that the reason India has been chosen for Francis' packaged odyssey is they have come to find their mother. Patricia Whitman was a notable absentee from their father's funeral, abandoning her sons to join a convent in the shadow of the Himalayas.

Here was the mystical India of Powell and Pressburger's nun classic *Black Narcissus* – a major touchstone for the designers, though Wales had doubled for Rajput-era India. Their convent scenes were shot the lusher

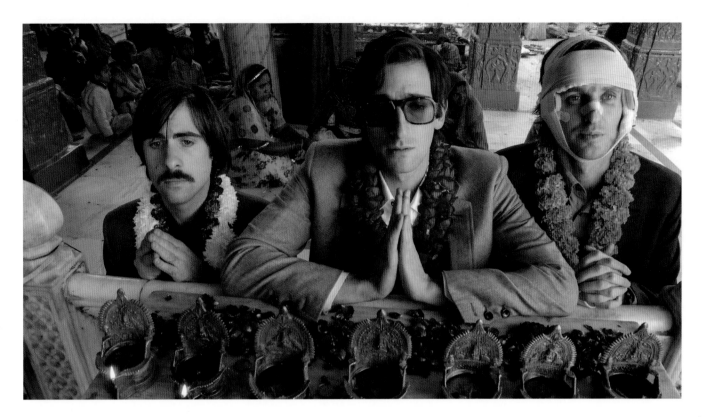

realm of Udaipur, in a former royal hunting lodge that once belonged to the Maharaja of Mewar, one of the Rajput-era rulers. You can imagine how much Anderson loved that.

According to the interconnected rules of the Anderson universe, the part of the dogmatic yet gentle Patricia had to be filled by Anjelica Huston, her hair cut boyishly short (close observers and Freudians will note that it matches the hairstyle of Portman's unreliable girlfriend in *Hotel Chevalier*).

Anderson had sent Huston a figurine of a nun, so she knew something was up. In fact, he sent her a second nun, having forgotten he'd sent the first. It was his way of piquing her interest.

With deep, mesmerizing, liquid eyes (the lighting is magnificently Powell and Pressburgerian), Patricia proves wise but otherwise non-

maternal. She warns her sons about a man-eating tiger loose in the vicinity (a touch of Rudyard Kipling for the mix). The next morning, she has flown again.

Like the jaguar shark roaming the deeps of *The Life Aquatic with Steve Zissou*, the tiger symbolises death. Once again, mortality – not least the recent death of the Whitmans' father in a car accident – lurks at the frayed edge of comedy. The film briefly leaves India to flashback to the brothers (in identical black suits) heading to his funeral in New York, stopping en route at a backstreet repair shop to claim his broken-down Porsche. Symbolically (of course), it has not been repaired yet.

Back in India, incremental changes have ganged up to bring about an alliance of Whitmans. Finally, they race for another train, the Bengal Lancer (a reference to

the 1935 drama *The Lives of a Bengal Lancer*). In a fittingly ironic epiphany not found anywhere on Francis' laminated list, in order to make it onboard the brothers have to discard the (emotional) baggage they have been lugging along with them all this way.

Only in a Wes Anderson film would those eleven matching tan leather cases, initialled and decorated with imprints of wild animals (by brother Eric Chase Anderson), be created by designer Marc Jacobs (who also made the Whitman suits) for fashion house Louis Vuitton. A few years later, Italian entrepreneur Alberto Favaretto launched a line of identical *Darjeeling Limited* cases, alongside Margot Tenenbaum iPhone cases, Team Steve Zissou trunks, and *Moonrise Kingdom* notebooks. He named his company 'Very Troubled Child'.

Above: Anderson directs
the first dinner scene on the
Darjeeling Limited – the train,
hired from an Indian railway
company, would effectively
become a moving studio.

Above: Shooting on location in Rajasthan, Anderson and his actors embraced the vibrancy of India, though the careful composition of the film's shots was never abandoned.

Despite the prestige of opening the New York Film Festival in September 2007, *The Darjeeling Limited* ended up ghettoized as a quirky, arthouse title, gaining little interest from the major awards ceremonies (this would be a prevailing problem for Anderson until *The Grand Budapest Hotel*). It was his smallest release since *Bottle Rocket*, leading to his smallest return since his first film: a disappointing $12 million. The studio's release jitters were perhaps a hangover from the extravagances of *The Life Aquatic with Steve Zissou*.

Reviews were respectful, but qualified. As with his previous film, what some critics once saw as distinctive was now disparaged as indulgent. What did this all add up to? It appeared that Anderson was in a Zissou-Whitman-like slump.

Like his previous adventure, this is a better film than its initial failure implies. Arguably, in fact, it is one of his finest. 'It has not only held up but gotten richer,' asserted Richard Brody in Anderson's favourite periodical, *The New Yorker*: 'Each viewing yields fresh wonders. Anderson's work resonates with the tension between artifice and nature; in *The Darjeeling Limited*, which was shot on location in India, often in places that defied directorial control, that tension is particularly fruitful.'[20]

This particular infusion of artifice with the real world resulted in a new, looser variation of the director's made-to-measure style. The emotions are more accessible; the metaphors more decipherable. 'There's a startling new maturity in *Darjeeling*, a compassion for the larger world,'[21] noticed Lisa Schwartzbaum in *Entertainment Weekly*. But with no loss of what fans (who took it straight to their hearts) loved about his films: that offbeat sensibility, that intricate design, those softly spoken themes.

The control-freak Whitman brothers (especially Francis) have to learn to relinquish control. Which is why you catch a glimpse of Anderson in every frame.

'When you're making a movie, you're not just organising the chaos, you're creating a new chaos which is the chaos of trying to make a movie,'[22] said Anderson. Every film is a documentary of its own making.

Amid the flurry of Indian locations, there is one beautifully idiosyncratic segment which takes us back into the embrace of Anderson's unique and captivating theatrical whims: the 'train of thought.'[23] In what could be construed as a dream sequence, the brothers are asked by their mother to express themselves 'without words.'[24] As this was a train movie, the metaphor came easily. The Whitmans collectively conceive of a sequence of sleeper compartments, each containing a

perfectly framed memory of their recent encounters and preoccupations: the orphans in the convent; the escaped cobra; the saved village boys; Peter's pregnant wife; et al.

'We searched for a while to figure out how to physically express it,' said Anderson. 'In the end, we took a train car, gutted it, and we built all these sets in the train car and then we set out into the desert on the train and we shot it live with this construction. A very odd thing.'[25]

There is no literal, matter-of-fact interpretation, only that it felt right: a necklace of self-contained sets, ending with an animatronic glimpse of the tiger – death appearing from the jungle. It was a vision of the entire film in miniature. Framed on the wall of the last compartment is a portrait of Satyajit Ray.

Natalie Portman came all the way to India to sit within a scaled-down train version of the *Hotel Chevalier* bedroom, and Bill Murray willingly returned for

Opposite: Wilson, Schwartzman and Brody all found the no-frills adventure of making a film in India a fulfilling experience. Life and art crossed over – they returned as changed men.

Right: A dash of Murray – Anderson's lucky star willingly took a tiny part as a mysterious American businessman. The director made it clear to his friend that he was a symbol. Of what, he didn't say.

a second tiny glimpse of his symbolic businessman, gazing out of the window, his feet up.

Which takes us back to that opening scene. For it is Murray we first see – as the American in a grey suit dashing through the thronging streets in a taxi, only to narrowly miss his train as Brody's Peter overtakes him on the platform, and leaps aboard, taking the story with him.

Anderson had asked his favourite actor more in hope than expectation. They had run into each other in New York, and Murray had enquired what the director was up to. Anderson mentioned India, the brothers, and then the crazy cameo he had in mind for him. 'It wasn't even a cameo,' he told him, 'more of a symbol.'

'A symbol?' responded Murray, entirely taken with the concept. 'I could do that.'[26]

He ended up coming to India on two separate occasions for a total of two minutes of screen time. Anderson had been inspired by a series of old American Express commercials featuring Karl Malden. 'We thought the Bill Murray character was working for an American Express type bureau,' explained Anderson. 'I don't think people really use those anymore – but we were calling it the Travellers' Exchange Bureau and he was the local representative, which probably meant he was in the CIA or something too.'[27]

Everybody, of course, was entitled to arrive at their own interpretation of the mysterious businessman. There is the connective tissue with Murray's place in Anderson's filmography, and a hint that he might be a ghost of the departed father. There is a look Peter gives him as he overtakes …

Make no mistake: this is an Anderson film. And Anderson was okay with that. 'I don't mind if my movies followed a certain train of thought over the course of them and if at the end they can sit on a shelf together.'[28]

However, after the flashes of realism in his last two films, Anderson would climb back beneath the security blanket of his fairy-tale whimsy. In fact, he was intent on taking it to new heights. Even as he promoted *The Darjeeling Limited*, he already had his next script written. As far as exotic locations were concerned, he was heading for England, or rather a fictional Home Counties England built in perfect miniature within the quiet, controllable confines of a London studio. His next film couldn't have been more of a contrast on nearly every level: he was adapting Roald Dahl's *Fantastic Mr. Fox* with stop-motion animation. And yet it felt every bit as much a Wes Anderson endeavour as his Indian epic.

FANTASTIC MR. FOX

The sixth film by Wes Anderson took an unusual turn – the actors were no more than twelve inches tall. In choosing to adapt Roald Dahl's blackly comic children's tale of a tailless fox he turned to stop-motion animation, but without losing any of his human insight

Wes Anderson sees no difference between real life and stop motion. Artistically speaking, that is. When he first dabbled in the medium in *The Life Aquatic with Steve Zissou*, he happily implied that rainbow-coloured plasticine seahorses belonged to the same universe as Bill Murray in a bobble hat. Anderson's approach to live action is so methodical and hyperrealistic that it might as well have been shot frame by frame. So, it seemed perfectly natural to make a full-length stop-motion enquiry into the fissured psychology of a suave fox.

'I'd been thinking about this one for ten years,'[1] said Anderson. He first read *Fantastic Mr Fox* as a child. Roald Dahl's novel (the book's title, unlike the film's, has no full stop after 'Mr') was one of his favourites, the first book he remembers owning, 'with my name written in the title page on a little sticker.'[2] So it wasn't so much that Anderson harboured some deep desire to make an animated movie; he wanted to pursue a stop-motion version of this particular book.

Dahl was a British novelist, born and raised in Wales, though his parents were Norwegian (a match for Anderson's Scandinavian heritage). He is celebrated for a set of darkly comic fantasies that interpret the vicissitudes of the world, or a peculiarly English pocket therein, from a child's perspective. His characters run to the eccentric and repellent – including a loathsome

husband and wife, The Twits, in his novel of the same name. *Charlie and the Chocolate Factory* is the most famous of his books, and not for nothing has Anderson's hermetic approach to filmmaking been compared to the psychedelic campus of confectioner extraordinaire Willy Wonka. Tim Burton – whose distinctive style in the face of studio conformity, and excursions into stop motion have drawn comparisons with Anderson – made a warped live-action blockbuster out of it in 2005. Stop-motion pioneer Henry Selick – the creator of the aquatic life of Anderson's earlier

Above left: *Fantastic Mr. Fox* was Wes Anderson's first animated movie, and his first-ever project to be (apparently) aimed at kids. It's also – to date – his only direct adaptation of someone else's work.

Above: Cool cats – the puppet gang step into action in a classic Anderson frame. Note that George Clooney's Mr. Fox, dead centre, wears a suit that matches those worn by his director.

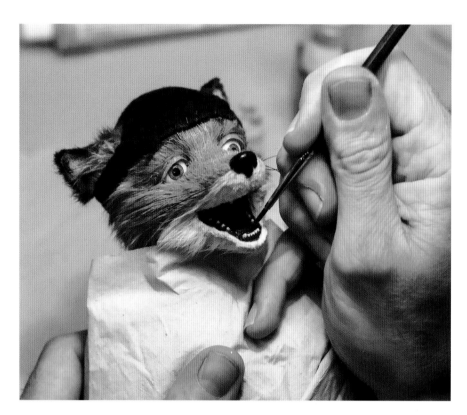

Left: The puppets were a wonderfully confounding mix of the rudimentary (especially when compared to CGI) and the highly expressive and intricate. They included joints made from Swiss watch parts.

Opposite: The Foxes (Clooney and Meryl Streep) get into something at bedtime. Note the painting behind them, one of Felicity Fox's portentous landscapes in oil, complete with ominous lightning bolt.

Below: Mr. Fox makes his case to a sceptical wife. Quite apart from its quotient of animal escapades, this was Anderson's first direct study of the intricacies of marriage.

film – had done a well-received stop-motion version of *James and the Giant Peach*. Early on, Selick was enrolled in Anderson's new venture, before leaving to direct *Coraline*.

Fantastic Mr. Fox, being a family saga, was much more Wes Anderson, and had the added advantage of never having previously been adapted. From certain angles, filming a Dahl book looked like a commercial move. Fox (the studio) felt so; they offered a budget of $40 million, confident this was a much easier sell than dejected brothers finding themselves in India.

But while he always sets out to find an audience, that isn't how Anderson's brain is wired. In the same vein as *Rushmore* and *The Life Aquatic with Steve Zissou*, he saw another story where 'the hero's personality is causing all the problems.'[3] Stop-motion foxes were the natural progression of his exploration of human nature.

The joke is, of course, that the animal characters are more human than the humans. They wear clothes over their fur. But they can still be found digging tunnels with windmilling arms – the scenes of animals making great escapes through the layer-cake of English soil have the madcap fury of *Looney Tunes* cartoons. Never having had any interest in the pop-daydream of CGI, Anderson wanted his animated world to actually exist, just as it did in his other films, but now completely handmade and doll-sized.

'Old-fashioned special effects tend to appeal to me.' Anderson wore it like a badge of honour, this determination to be out-of-step with his times. 'There's an imperfection that doesn't really qualify as an imperfection, because it's the real thing.'[4]

As a result of his approach, Anderson's cast of puppet animals in dapper clothes, with marbles for eyes,

have the appealingly lo-fi look of the soulful puppets in Oliver Postgate's children's serials of the British seventies such as *The Clangers* and *Bagpuss*. The medium also resonated with Dahl's bric-à-brac charms.

What makes *Fantastic Mr. Fox* so delightful is not the breathtaking precision of the animation, but how cunningly it conveys character and a deviant version of modern life. It is a sublime marriage of script and technique. And unlike live action, with its human limitations, with stop motion Anderson could think things up on the spot (which would bring its own obsessions). But first he needed to acquire a Dahl frame of mind. This was, after all, Anderson's first, and to date his only direct adaptation.

Anderson chose again to collaborate with Noah Baumbach. Marriage, family, droll wildlife: this was the co-writer of *The Life Aquatic With Steve Zissou's* forte. And following Anderson's fruitful immersion into the inkwell of India with *The Darjeeling Limited*, he bade Baumbach join him in Great Missenden, the quaint village nestled in England's Chiltern Hills where Roald Dahl had lived and worked. Indeed, following some very polite correspondence with Dahl's widow Felicity ahead of time, they gained unfettered access to his home, Gipsy House, and its rustic grounds, including the luxuriant shed with a canary yellow door in which the author plied his magic, which had been preserved like a museum piece. Anderson was given permission to sit in his old armchair and write, hoping to channel Dahl's flights of fantasy and caustic humour – an exact replica of Dahl's den, down to the mug of pencils on his desk, would be provided for Mr. Fox's office. The tree the Foxes inhabit was based on the striking beech in the garden of Gispy House.

To an extent, Anderson based the character of Mr. Fox on Dahl. At an abstract level, he said, this was 'about him as much as the book.'[5] Anderson read all Dahl's books and autobiographies, and got to leaf through the many sketches he made configuring his hero's movements like storyboards. Mrs. Fox turns out to be named Felicity.

They would spent two months in England, between writing sessions, going for long, mulchy walks in the countryside, taking Polaroids of the scenery and locals to be used as reference for their ersatz idyll to come, complete with a suburban railway artery the size of a train set (with stop motion, Orson Welles' adage about the joys of filmmaking is fulfilled).

While on the one hand the film is the story of a conceited, chicken-stealing fox, whose over-confidence almost brings ruin to his family and the local animal community, it is evidently one of Anderson's mannered odes to crackpot families made up of neurotics and nitwits. Pompous fathers, long-suffering mothers, dysfunctional offspring, and bumbling neighbours are concealed beneath orangeade fur.

Anderson and Baumbach stick to the bones of Dahl's English-teashop comedy of bad animal manners, but slyly divert and expand the antics to probe the fraying Fox family. As Baumbach explained, they took the book as their middle chapter and expanded in both directions, elaborating on elements only sketched in the book, developing backstories for characters, inventing new ones. Above all, they were amplifying the relationships.

Mr. Fox, unable (or unwilling) to put a curb on his wild side, will still lose his tail to a gunshot in a poorly planned series of raids on the chicken coops of farmers Boggis, Bunce and Bean. But deep down, this is another audit on dysfunctional family life in the midst of chaos (largely caused by the hubris

Opposite: The yellow front door to Roald Dahl's 'shed', located in the tree-lined grounds of his Buckinghamshire home Gipsy House, where he hid himself away to write his magical stories.

Right: Anderson's use of autumnal hues imbued Dahl's English Home Counties setting with a feel of fantasy. Note the borderline two-dimensional nature of the frame.

Below: In the wake of Mr. Fox-fuelled calamity, the animals rally round. Anderson's interests were widening to include an individual's effects on an entire community.

of Mr. Fox himself, whose braggadocio is delivered by the honeyed tones of George Clooney). A strained marriage will come into focus with the alarmingly prescient Mrs. Fox (Meryl Streep, continuing where Anjelica Huston left off) trying to tame her husband, who is also struggling to connect with his insecure cub Ash (Jason Schwartzman). This later situation is exacerbated by the arrival of his cousin, Kristofferson (Eric Chase Anderson), who is everything Ash is not: charming, athletic, funny and an ace at Whack-Bat, the sport invented by Anderson for the occasion. Despite explanatory on-screen diagrams, the game, centred on whacking a burning pine cone, remains perfectly incomprehensible and is clearly a parody of cricket.

Anderson and Baumbach's expansion of the book gained its own internal logic. If they were to show the Foxes first buying their upscale 'tree house' they would therefore need a real estate agent – Stan Weasel (voiced by Anderson, no less), who despite the general seventies aura possesses a mobile phone. QED: every grown animal needed a job. So it was that two fully grown filmmakers, Anderson and Baumbach, would have serious discussions about how they would need an attorney to advise on the deal, and how he should be a badger (of Badger, Beaver & Beaver) with the wheedling voice of Bill Murray.

The script evolved in the opposite direction of the usual Anderson storytelling, whereby adult concerns

Above: There was something about the design of the puppets that always hinted at the actor behind them. We can see Bill Murray's exasperated expressions in Mr. Badger …

Opposite: … and Willem Dafoe's taut cheekbones in the cider-addicted, knife-wielding Rat, who comes with a delightfully incongruent Louisiana drawl.

were implanted with childlike whimsicality: boats, trains, striped mice, man-eating tigers, and the like. While set in a compartment of essentially storybook England, tonally the film has a lot in common with the quick-fire comedies of Preston Sturges and Howard Hawks. It is a bona fide comedy, but not without its wounded side. Beneath its twee exterior was planted a brazenly American sensibility of psychobabbling togetherness.

They were moving away from Dahl, while always staying true to him. Which, claimed Anderson, was why it helped so much that they had decided that Mr. Fox *is* Dahl. They would ask themselves: 'What would Dahl do if he were not writing this but stealing these chickens?'[6] With a Dahl orientation, the writers developed a sideline in ludicrous animal lore. Beagles love blueberries! Foxes are mildly allergic to linoleum! And there was always that Anderson genius for incongruous detail: a rat (voiced by Willem Dafoe with a New Orleans twang) who guards a cider cellar dances like one of the delinquents from *West Side Story*, twirling a switchblade.

Anderson noticed that the wild-animal metaphor became more and more prominent; the strange irony of 'this guy in corduroy,' (as Anderson described his leading fox), 'who doesn't want to lose contact with his wildness.'[7] The vision of a lone wolf at the climax of the movie, not to be found in Dahl's pages, became, 'for some reason,'[8] the key image for the director.

He became less and less concerned with whether he was making an adult film with puppets or a children's film with life lessons. It became 'the thing it was meant to be,'[9] he said, instinctually creating another film that slipped between definitions.

A wonderful example of how the film danced between adult and children's concerns is the conversion of all cuss words to exactly that – the word 'cuss'. To wit: Mr. Fox getting into a slanging match with his usually mild-mannered attorney. 'If you're gonna cuss with somebody,' growls Mr. Badger, 'you're not gonna cuss with me, you little cuss!'[10] There is the baring of teeth.

Five films to the good, preparing to shoot a sixth, we have reached the midway point in Anderson's career thus far. Which seems a fittingly symmetrical moment to take stock.

So, a brief status report: like Woody Allen or even Stanley Kubrick, and more recently the likes of the Coens, Quentin Tarantino, and to a degree Tim Burton, Anderson was established on a relatively safe ledge in Hollywood. As long as he kept his budgets under control, he could go about his singular business without commercial pressures. He was now a recognized artist, with an eager and expectant audience. That said, after two poorly performing films, questions were being raised in cultural circles. Was there such a thing as too much Wes Anderson? Critics had been mounting one of their mandated backlashes. He was being derided as a hipster director in an Age of Twee. Commentator Christian Lorentzen wrote an entire essay entitled *Captain Neato: Wes Anderson and the Problem with Hipsters; Or, What Happens When a Generation Refuses to Grow Up* in the journal *n+1* (which sounds like a pretty hipster publication). Where was the narrative thrust, they grumbled? Didn't all this arch stylization amount to little more than an assemblage of fetish objects?

Anderson was unrepentant. He was now making an entire film out of fetish objects (many covered in fur). At the same time, this was an adaptation of a best-selling author, which would result in his most traditional, fast-paced, joke-rich piece of storytelling. He wanted to have it all his own way: to straddle genres, to make highly personal films, to probe human frailty, and have rip-roaring comic-book adventures wherein an intrepid – not-to-say debonair – fox will lose his tail (puffed-up symbol for his pride) to a vindictive farmer who wears it as a necktie. Anderson was

determined that his blend of reality and artifice should 'end up being a combination that is not quite one thing or the other, but is its own thing.'[11]

Take, for instance, the accents. Voice-casting many of his favourite actors (by now a ragtag company), with the addition of new personnel in Clooney and Streep to 'make sure'[12] he stayed on his toes, Anderson wanted them to maintain their natural American accents.

'We'd written the characters as Americans, without meaning to, so if an English person talked that way, it would have sounded silly,' he explained. 'So our rule was that all the animals spoke like Americans – because having talking animals is already a fairly significant break with reality! The humans have British accents. Although one guy, a helicopter pilot, is South African.'[13]

Rather than the usual schedule of studio sessions based around actor

Above: In some senses, stop-motion offered Anderson the perfect directorial conditions. He could stay in control literally frame by frame.

Opposite: While Anderson strove for seamless storytelling, he didn't want perfection. There was comic value if the audience noticed when the scale of the puppets changed.

availability and location, Anderson went out of his way to record as many of his voice cast as naturally as possible. Before production they took up residence in a remote Connecticut farm, where they acted out the story. He likened it to a radio play.

'We went out in a forest, we went in an attic, we went in a stable,' recalled a delighted director. 'We went underground for some things. There was a great spontaneity in the recordings because of that, I think.'[14]

There is documentary evidence of superstar Clooney skipping round the farmyard and rooting about in the woods. He was another trooper 'up for anything,'[15] said Anderson, and was committing himself physically to the animal-gentleman cross-stitch of Mr. Fox's temperament. And who can deny that there is an echo of the handsome star of the *Ocean's Eleven* films (doubly signalled by Mr. Fox enrolling Wallace Wolodarsky's Kylie Sven Opossum and Eric Chase Anderson's Kristofferson

Silverfox into his extra-legal schemes) in the look of Mr. Fox's pliable puppet and his silky movements?

Meanwhile, in a Paris studio, to supplement Alexandre Desplat's score, former Britpop mainstay Jarvis Cocker provided the thematically tilted *Petey's Song*, as well as giving Sheffield-inflected voice to banjo-playing, folk-singing puppet Pete. He was a friend from Paris, and at one stage had been set to narrate the entire film.

As was his usual practice, Anderson provided piles of storyboards and sketches for every scene, reassuringly neat stick-people (or stick-fox) diagrams of camera moves often drawn on hotel stationery. In one sublimely meta joke, on the wall of Mr. Fox's study is a miniature simulacrum of the cue cards for scenes pinned to the production office wall.

The puppets came care of specialists Mackinnon & Saunders, who sound like they were dreamed up by Anderson, but were in fact the proud Greater Manchester-based firm responsible for creating the stars of everything from *Postman Pat* to Tim Burton's *Corpse Bride*. They used plasticine, fibreglass, and Swiss-watch parts (for the joints), to meet the director's fastidious demands.

These were actors he could design like props. It took seven months for Anderson to be satisfied with the look of Mr. Fox, who came in six different sizes. He enlisted artist Donald Chaffin, who had illustrated the first edition of the book (the one Anderson owned), to provide concept art. Sour-faced Franklin Bean (a mix of Dahl, voice actor Michael Gambon and something Richard Harris had once worn on the *David Letterman Show*) required fifteen coats of paint before Anderson was satisfied with his pallid complexion. To knit the woolly jumper of the cider-guzzling Rat, they had to whittle miniature knitting needles. The director demanded real fur for his animals: in stop motion, the responsibly sourced fur from goats and kangaroos had this lifelike way of ruffling like the hackles of real animals.

In all, 535 puppets were made. It was the opposite of adjusting to the limits of location; everything was so controllable, and that in itself was maddening. There was always this sense he could improve on something. As producer Jeremy Dawson said of Anderson, he is a 'real director of props.'[16]

The miniature sets were every bit as detailed as the full-sized variation. But now, on the hushed soundstages at 3 Mills Studios on the eastern fringes of London, Anderson had thirty different units at work simultaneously: trees, fields, tunnels, farmhouses, factories, cellars, a supermarket and a twenty-foot long city street modelled on Bath, unified by the autumnal palate he had set for the film. The water was made from clingfilm, flames from slivers of Pears soap, and the resulting smoke is cotton wool.

There are Anderson touches that are entirely his own. His love of analogue gizmos and kitsch relics is found in chunky black-and-white television sets, clunking Dictaphones, record players, and bikes with seventies-style banana seats. If this were to be a children's film then it would inevitably reflect the childhood Anderson experienced. Seventies-style nostalgia is written into every frame.

Animating it all was a test of patience like nothing he had ever experienced. Effectively, it took two years to shoot the film – Baumbach completed two live-action films in the meantime. This quaint model universe was creeping to life at around six seconds every two days.

Right: Working for scale – Mr. Badger's Murray pretends to nap while visiting the production at 3 Mills Studios in London, revealing a *Gulliver's Travels* contrast between actor and street set.

Here's the thing. Given the painstaking processes of stop-motion animation, that would in real terms allow him little participation once animation was underway, Anderson chose to direct as much as he could from his apartment in Paris. Utilizing modern communications technology – ironically, for a film so determinedly analogue in its style, state-of-the-art Apple software would be required for Anderson to monitor the production from afar – he could have real-time access to individual frames, sending and answering hundreds of emails per day. It was like he was conducting these musicians, said Dawson, 'by remote.'[17] Anderson would even film himself acting out scenes on his iPhone, then send them over as reference. There was no let-up in Anderson's effort – he barely left his desk – but this long-distance romance became the source of some controversy when

cinematographer Tristan Oliver was quoted in the *Los Angeles Times* wondering if his director was a 'little O.C.D.'[18] preferring to spend his day locked inside a room with a computer.

'It was a drag,'[19] commented Anderson through gritted teeth.

Anderson had made his longed-for move to Paris in 2005, taking a roomy apartment in Montmartre. The city was everything he'd hoped for. He would watch films in the Latin Quarter revival houses; the first thing he saw there was *The Pink Panther*, a repeat of his very first cinema outing as a child in Houston. He was always looking back. It was here that he wrote the first draft of *The Darjeeling Limited*, a tale of brothers much like his own. Co-writer Jason Schwartzman ended up staying for two months, as though he and Anderson were *The Odd Couple*. The filmmaker would split his time between Paris and New York. 'The difference between exile

and nomadism is probably just your mood,'[20] he shrugged.

A year into production, Anderson's beloved magazine *The New Yorker* arrived in Paris to profile an artist abroad, lifting the lid on a world exactly as we might expect it to be. His home was arrayed like one of his sets. An Art Deco desk with seventies touch-tone telephone; bookcases filled with art tomes, encyclopaedias, and matching sets of classics; weatherworn leather cases; a postcard of Albert Camus ... all set off against yellow walls and curtains.

The point is his films are so personal they actually resemble his life (or his life resembles them). The brown, corduroy suit sported by Mr. Fox was made by Anderson's personal tailor (a luxury afforded by success). The director had a matching one made at the same time.

The New Yorker accompanied Anderson on one of his periodic

Above: The sets might have been tiny but there was no letup in Andersonian detail. Here, in Mr. Badger's office, Mr. Fox pauses before a shelf of legal tomes and a painting of his lawyer's forebadgers.

Opposite above: The trio of villainous farmers, Boggis (Robin Hurlstone), Bean (Michael Gambon) and Bunce (Hugo Guinness). These bad guys were given the appropriate English accents, while the heroic animals spoke in American enunciation.

Right: Mr. Fox (Clooney) and his extra-textual opossum best friend Kylie (Wallace Wolodarsky) plot a forthcoming heist. There was plenty of Dahl, as well as both Clooney and Anderson, in the portrayal of the leading fox.

visits to 3 Mills Studios, watching the director confer with his puppeteers in person. He pressed them to pursue reality, however small. Studying the supermarket set, the tiny shelves filled with tiny groceries, Anderson informed producer Jeremy Dawson, 'Stores don't put bread in the refrigerator.' Maybe they do here, Dawson quipped. 'I'm saying a serious thing,' responded Anderson. 'Maybe we shouldn't have bread in the refrigerator.'[21] This was micro-micromanagement.

And yet, with the closed-off nature of each scene, Owen Wilson (who voices Coach Skip) was startled to see a director, usually the dynamo of the production, idling for an hour with nothing immediate to do. Anderson confessed that initially he had often been caught at a loss, unable to channel his creative energies, which certainly contributed to the realization he could do much of his directing from home.

He conceived of shots (in person or via his polished Apple Pro set-up) just as he would with flesh-and-blood actors. No concessions were made to the fact he was dealing with puppets, and emphasis was given to performance through long takes and close-ups. This was counterintuitive for a team of animators taught to keep things moving for fear the spell will be broken. To Anderson's thinking, the magic is in bringing the dance between life and filmmaking closer to the camera. He was willing to keep a puppet perfectly still in the frame, not even blinking. To stop the stop motion to allow a character to think. What production designer Nelson Lowry called 'a compression of character.'[22] So taken are we with the characters we willingly suspend disbelief. We can hear the puppets thinking.

What this time-lapse filmmaking also allowed was the ability to tinker with the story, inventing new scenes,

Above: Anderson attending the premiere. After two fulfilling but painfully slow years of production, he found he was more than ready to return to real life. Or, at least, his version of it.

rewriting existing ones, adjusting his narrative in ways he could never hope to do in the conventional live arena. The willing cast would be corralled back in a studio to record new lines. 'So while it seems more rigid,' he appreciated, 'you actually get two passes at that spontaneity.'[23] In effect, the film was edited as they went along, and he could go back and re-stage an individual frame if it didn't pass muster.

Utilizing notes he found in Dahl's archive, Anderson altered the ending of the book for a more upbeat message. On the page, the animals end up exiled underground beneath the farmer's

storehouses, safe from the clutches of nature and the predatory farmers, but with their true wild selves finally hemmed in. On film, they disco in herky-jerky delight that they have found a new way to live underneath the supermarket. In their hermetic world, with ready resources to hand, anything is possible.

Opening on 8 October 2009, to a gush of career-best reviews, *Fantastic Mr. Fox* should have done better. The resulting $46 million worldwide was chicken feed. It is a lovely, vibrant film, at once Andersonian in voice, while funny and charming well beyond the arthouse underground.

Was its tone too old-school to attract new kids? Was stop motion too moth-eaten in the face of CGI trinkets? Did Dahl's coal-black humour – and Anderson's determination to cut against political correctness – no longer register? The fact of the matter was that *Fantastic Mr. Fox* was greeted as a Wes Anderson film; a winning formula for devoted fans, but one with no escape from the label of arrested adolescence.

However, as Christopher Orr said in the *New Republic*, this animated movie was a 'modest miracle'[24] of invention. Here was an Anderson fable that held hipster irony and childlike pleasure in the telling of tales in perfect balance.

Of course, he had hoped for a bigger audience, but Anderson was content with his stop motion. 'I now have that experience,' he said. 'I have something in my arsenal as a moviemaker I can use – I don't know how long it will last.'[25] He wasn't done with the medium yet, but for now he would return to real life, however artificial. Indeed, his next two films turned out more animated than ever before. The fur had rubbed off on him.

Above: The root cause of their problems – a gaggle of infuriated animals turn on Mr. Fox, in his prison-bar pyjamas, while his nephew Kristofferson (Eric Chase Anderson) and son Ash (Jason Schwartzman) look on.

MOONRISE KINGDOM

For his seventh film, Wes Anderson turned to romance. Only the couple in question are two troubled twelve-year-old runaways, who live on a small island off the coast of New England, with a symbolic storm on its way

When he was twelve years old, Wes Anderson fell in love. The object of his affection was a girl in his class, sat two rows over and three seats up. He can remember exactly, though they never spoke. He never dared. To this day, she remains unaware of his longings. Or that she was the inspiration for a movie.

Years later, Anderson – happy in a long-term relationship with Lebanese writer, illustrator, and knitwear designer Juman Malouf – was asked by a French reporter if *Moonrise Kingdom* was based on a memory of a fantasy. It was a very French question. 'At first, I wasn't quite sure what that meant,' admitted Anderson. 'Then I realized that that is exactly what the movie is.'[1]

Falling in love when you're twelve was so sudden and inexplicable it could be overwhelming. 'It just sort of blindsides you,'[2] he remembered. At that age you could be so invested in a book that it becomes your whole world. Children, he said, 'have this overpowering need for fantasy.'[3] In other words, love is like running away to another world.

Which sounds like a manifesto for all of Anderson's films: elaborate fantasies made from real emotion. However, in this case, rather than a character or characters or a setting, he started out by wanting to explore that emotion. Or, as he put it, 'a memory of an emotion that I was hoping to re-create in some way.'[4]

Moonrise Kingdom was a return to the romantic impulses of *Rushmore*, only in an even more rarified setting. The year is an unusually precise 1965, the place a fictional island off the coast of New England named New Penzance, a realm as rich and preposterous as any in the Anderson atlas. Shot on location, the film possesses a lush, outdoorsy vitality. This time, Anderson's lovebirds are well matched in age. At the heart of the story are two twelve-year-old runaways. Book-crazy Suzy Bishop (Kara Hayward) is fleeing a fraying home where her lawyer parents (Bill Murray and Frances McDormand)

Above: Lovers on the run (kinda) – Suzy Bishop (Kara Hayward) and Sam Shakusky (Jared Gilman) get their bearings. On the inverted island of *Moonrise Kingdom,* the youngsters are the most knowing and adult figures.

Opposite: While all of Wes Anderson's films nostalgically hark back to bygone eras, this playful romance was the first to be firmly set in the specific year of 1965, when America still held on to its innocence.

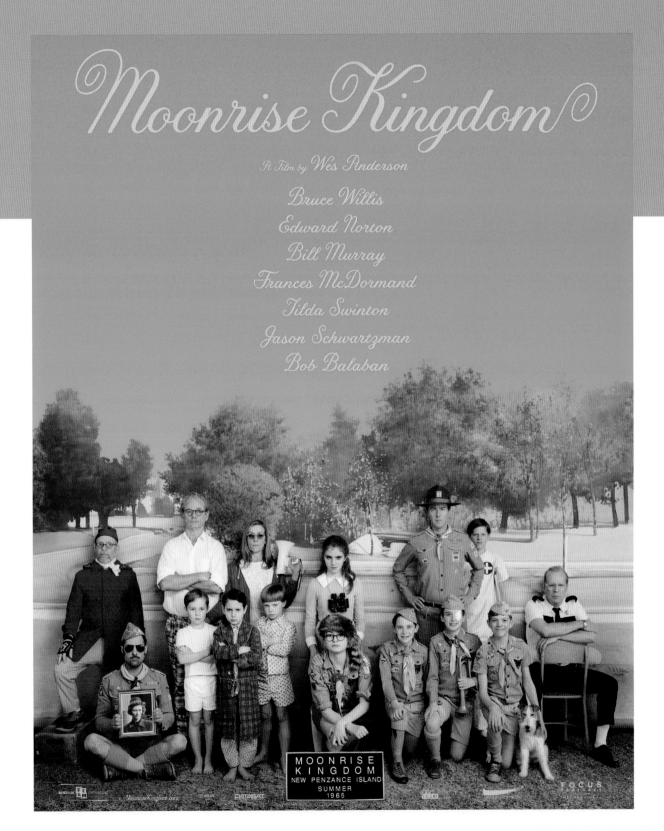

sleep in separate beds. Khaki Scout Sam Shakusky (Jared Gilman), an orphan surplus to requirements with his foster family, is AWOL from Camp Ivanhoe, with its regimen of morning inspections and outdoor pursuits. On their trail comes a muddle of despondent parents, wisecracking rival scouts, a glum local police chief (Bruce Willis), and a fearsome representative of authority in a blue bonnet known only as Social Services (portrayed, with an immaculately menacing hint of brimstone, by Tilda Swinton).

As we've encountered previously, Anderson suspects that most adults, drained of passion, slip back into childishness (as often expressed by Murray's slumped shoulders). One of the sublime charms of his adorable seventh film is that even though its protagonists are only dipping their toes into puberty, they count among the director's most mature creations. As Anthony Lane observed in his glowing review in *The New Yorker*, 'Anderson's great gift is to catch the generations as they intersect.'[5] He recalled Gene Hackman as Royal Tenenbaum, perched on the tailgate of a garbage truck with his grandsons.

In preparation, Anderson returned to the wellspring of his favourite books and movies in search of the textures of pre-adolescent angst. François Truffaut, never far from his thoughts, provided two masterful paeans to the freedoms and sorrows of juvenile delinquency in *The 400 Blows* and *Small Change*. He also cited Ken Loach's *Black Jack* and Waris Hussein's *Melody* (written by Alan Parker) – both upbeat social-realist depictions of youth hankering for adulthood. Orphanhood, of course, has been a longstanding emotional hook for both book and film. On the first page of Roald Dahl's *James and the Giant Peach* (adapted by Anderson's friend Henry Selick), a rhino eats the hero's parents.

The other significant influence was classical music. Anderson had been taken with the idea of recreating British composer Benjamin Britten's one-act opera *Noye's Fludde* (whose words are based on a 15th-century mystery play about Noah's Ark). Intended for children to perform, it conveys a tumultuous storm, using ingenious musical effects. He and his older brother Mel had been in a local production when he was ten, and Britten's music unfailingly returned him to that time in his life.

He imagined Suzy and Sam meeting backstage at a rehearsal for a community production. These two characters are 'hit by a thunderbolt and determined to act on it,'[6] he said. The retelling of the Noah's Ark story would spread through the film, with a storm – both meteorological and metaphorical – forecast for the finale.

'One idea connects to the other and you start to stitch it together,' said Anderson. 'I thought, "Let's keep doing

Above: At first, Anderson had to coax performances from inexperienced leads, but as the shoot progressed he marvelled at how Hayward and Gilman took ownership of their characters.

Opposite above: If the kids are growing up fast, the adult population – mainly Mr. Bishop (Bill Murray), Mrs. Bishop (Frances McDormand), Scout Master Ward (Edward Norton in shorts) and Captain Sharp (Bruce Willis) – are determinedly heading in the other direction.

Britten." So I started listening to more and more Britten and we ended up with several other pieces.'7

The film opens with excerpts (played on a portable record player) from Britten's *Young Person's Guide to the Orchestra*. This educational composition, whose recording Anderson also owned as a boy, reveals how the various layers of a composition come together. It was art commenting on art, and Anderson liked how it worked as a metaphor for the way a movie works. 'Or something like that,'8 he shrugged.

The soundtrack combines the august reverberations of Britten with the melodious crooning of Hank Williams, which after some experimentation proved to be on the ideal wavelength for Willis's blunted Captain Sharp.

The script, said Anderson, 'took a year of trying to write, and then a month of actually getting it written.'9 He had started out on his own, figuring

out what he thought it was supposed to be. Then he joined forces with Roman Coppola and it fell into place very quickly. Among Coppola's telling contributions is McDormand's Laura shrieking instructions to her disorderly brood via a bullhorn, something his own mother, Eleanor Coppola, did to corral her offspring.

A quick digression on scripts: 'For me, when I make a script, I'm also kind of obsessively working on a script that's a thing for somebody to read,'10 explained Anderson, referring to the typescript he finally hands over to his actors and crew. The screenplay for an Anderson provides descriptions for things only hinted at on screen. He often inserts photographs and other visual references. The idea is to make sure his cast- or crew-member can sit there and *'experience'*11 the story. Later, Anderson willingly publishes his scripts to vouch for their stand-alone literary value.

Whatever the circumstances of his career might be, *Moonrise Kingdom* re-enforced Anderson's place as a consummate filmmaker. It is an impeccable film only he could make. But trailing a trio of box office failures, he had to be economical. The studios were not forthcoming. Focus Films, a division of Universal, would pick up the film for distribution (giving it the backing of studio marketing), but this counts as his only true independent film, and Anderson had to make a meagre budget of $16 million stretch to contain his flood of ideas.

Above: The Khaki Scouts play on a classic screen tradition of wiseacre G.I.s in everything from *The Phil Silvers Show* to *From Here to Eternity*. Meanwhile, a love of fireworks recalls Dignan from *Bottle Rocket*.

First of all, *Moonrise Kingdom* marked a return to America, though still a thousand miles from any prefabricated Hollywood definition of it. The film doesn't even make it to the mainland. Sealed off from reality, New Penzance Island is as prescribed as the genteel England of *Fantastic Mr. Fox*. Anderson and Coppola even drew their own map of it, keen to fix its geographical features with precision, like scouts. In the movie, we will glimpse maps, charts, and local weather reports.

Why an island? Well, Anderson wanted somewhere the audience had never been. He pictured a place suffused with magic, like Peter Pan's Never Never Land, with its tribe of lost boys. 'The girl is carrying around a suitcase full of fantasy books,' he explained. 'Somewhere along the way, I started to feel like the movie should feel like it could be in that suitcase. That it could be one of those books.'[12]

As with every foray into the creative space of this Texan dreamer, fable mingles with fact. A real island had nudged his imagination. Named Naushon, it lies off the shore of Massachusetts. His friend, erstwhile actor Wally Wolodarsky (who had recently voiced Kylie the opossum in *Fantastic Mr. Fox*) lived there, and local ordinances prevented any modern housing or the use of cars. It had an enchanted quality, rather like a Wes Anderson movie.

Why 1965? Well, Anderson conceived of a storyteller who would address the audience directly, breaking the fourth wall. Except, contrary to the charmed atmosphere, he would be a matter-of-fact meteorologist framing the entire tale within a scientific documentary (with hints of Steve Zissou's *métier*) and deadpanned by Bob Balaban. He might also be God, clad in a scarlet duffle coat. The prevailing weather is of great import: that tempest is due, with its Shakespearean and Biblical

ramifications, but there is a localized depression lurking over the adult population of New Penzance.

The choice of Balaban came with its own complex pedigree: he had appeared in Steven Spielberg's *Close Encounters of the Third Kind* as a cartographer (a map maker!) alongside Anderson-hero Truffaut, two scientists exploring alien visitations, echoing Suzy's taste in fiction. What's more, Balaban had published a diary of his experiences on Spielberg's epic, one of those filmmaking histories Anderson had lapped up as a student, whose succinct tone of voice he wanted to reproduce at the fringes of *Moonrise Kingdom*.

'The first paragraph I wrote for him, I just spontaneously wrote, "The year is 1965,"' he recalled. 'I hadn't really intended it. It was sort of a spontaneous moment. I do think that the scouts and its Norman Rockwell-type of Americana is sort of part of it.'[13]

This was the first Anderson film that was actively a period piece – not that it made a huge difference.

Anderson and his team used Google Earth for their first location scout. They were seeking a specific coastline, the right kind of wildlife, a certain bucolic mood. They found it in Rhode Island, on the Atlantic coast of leafy New England. And through the summer of 2011, they would shuttle between coves, woods, regional Episcopalian churches, and the readymade Yawgoog Scout Reservation to assemble their love-struck island.

Swayed by his recent venture in stop motion, Anderson drew and edited together storyboards ahead of time, even recording a soundtrack to go with his animatic. Here was a director exerting ever more control over his medium, building entire sets to facilitate certain shots. The perfect exterior for Suzy's clapboard house was found in the Thousand Islands area of the Canadian border then rebuilt in Rhode Island, with

the interior constructed in a former *Linens 'n Things* store outside Newport. The set was laid out horizontally, so he could dolly between rooms and through walls as he had with train carriages in *The Darjeeling Limited*, connecting his lost souls together.

For all the treasure trove of detail and geometry, the story lived and breathed through its young leads, whose romance stirs via flashback in the church hall dressing room of *Noye's Fludde*. It's a classic Anderson set-up, a story within the story (an opera within the opera), with the junior cast members dressed as animals, suggesting he hadn't quite shaken the zoological orientation of his previous assignment (Suzy is a raven). Like Max Fischer's plays in *Rushmore*, the opera's lavish staging makes it an Anderson production in miniature, an in-joke about his theatrical methods.

As he had with the search for Max, Anderson set aside the time for auditions in full faith that the perfect couple would appear. Now though, it was important he have no preconceived ideas of how they looked. Jason Schwartzman looked nothing like the willowy young Jagger he imagined for Max, but he was absolutely right. They met with hundreds before Sam and Suzy walked in.

Gilman and Hayward had done nothing more than school productions. 'They're relatively unknown outside of their seventh grade classrooms,'[14] quipped Anderson. Gilman first, then Hayward, both equally spontaneous, were cast at their initial auditions. To keep things as loose and unintimidating as possible, for their scenes Anderson reduced his crew to the bare bones. Which was its own challenge if you needed thirty feet of dolly track in a sleepy wood with the weather coming in.

For the montage of the pair travelling through the wilderness, Anderson began with a pre-shoot shoot, using a documentary-sized crew of three and a camera no bigger than a shoebox. The kids picked things up pretty quickly, letting their imagination roam like their counterparts.

Both characters are strangely familiar. Suzy reminds you of the young Margot Tenenbaum. She has the same urge to write, the same broken home, the same penetrating gaze through smeared mascara, though less of the nihilism and more of a temper (where her mother is concerned). There is a recurring image of Suzy scanning the horizon through binoculars. It was an image Anderson found in Satyajit Ray's drama *The Lonely Wife*, about a secluded wife who falls for her cousin. And in *Rear Window*: the most famous of voyeuristic pictures, the first Hitchcock he can remember seeing, and his mother's favourite film.

You will have gathered that Suzy reads voraciously, and is symbolically

Opposite: Suzy (Hayward) and Sam (Gilman) scheme with Khaki Scout slick Cousin Ben (Jason Schwartzman). Like Schwartzman before them in *Rushmore*, the two young stars were neophytes who took complete ownership of their characters.

Right: Throughout the film, Suzy is defined by how she observes the island's goings-on via binoculars. She is that most symbolic of movie figures: the voyeur.

Below: Suzy scans the horizon for signs of her loved one from the top of the lighthouse at Summer's End – the town's name referencing not only the end of childhood for the protagonists but for America as a whole.

devoted to fantasy. The suitcase she's been lugging turns out to be full of purloined library books. Anderson and Coppola made up their own titles like *The Girl from Jupiter* and *Shelly and the Secret Universe*. When a gang of scouts catch up with the fugitives, Suzy turns mother, reading them passages as Wendy does in *Peter Pan*.

Parentless, an island unto himself, Sam takes charge of their getaway with his ready supply of tent, BB gun, canoe, hot dogs, scouting skills, and plucky bravado. He's a less highly strung version of Max or Francis Whitman from *The Darjeeling Limited*. Taking one rueful look at Suzy's less-than-mobile library, he gives the most Andersonian of responses: 'Some of those are going to be overdue.'[15] They are now officially a couple on the lam. It's another absurd take on genre: *Gun Crazy*, *Bonnie and Clyde*, and *Badlands* blended with *Swallows and Amazons*.

It's them against the world (or this island full of misfits anyway). What works so beautifully is that on one level the couple are enacting a pastiche of falling in love (born out of movies they really shouldn't have seen yet). On the other hand they are definitely in love, but playing it by ear.

The film's unspoken title is the name they write in the sand of the secret cove where they make camp, a kingdom of two. Here Anderson daringly introduces the possibility of underage sexual stirrings. Or, at least, some heavy petting. They try a kiss and a small amount of touching in their underwear. There would, inevitably, be rumblings about Anderson going a step too far, but the sweetness and sensitivity with which he handles the scene keeps it honest. There is a stoic determination that this is what they are *supposed* to be doing, the pleasures still vague. Still, the piercing of Suzy's ear with a fishhook, a green beetle dangling decorously

from its end, serves as a clear enough metaphor. This is a turning point.

Never has the inverted world of Anderson been so acutely observed, and never has it lodged so swiftly in our hearts. The children reach for magic, while the adults are lost to disenchantment. The Bishops are on the downslope of a marriage; McDormand's fussy Laura, having embarked on an empty affair with Captain Sharp,

leaves Murray to plumb new depths of comic despair as Walt, sunken husband and outraged father. 'Our daughter's been abducted by one of these beige lunatics!'[16] he rails to the universe, as if it's his fate to lose both mother and daughter to men in uniform.

Anderson's admiration of McDormand's work with the Coens meant that she was on his most-wanted list. And for good reason: she brings

Above: Violent couple-on-the-lam classic *Bonnie and Clyde* and its ilk served as a tangential inspiration for the movie, with Suzy and Sam pursued across the island.

Left: After an extensive search, which began with Google Earth, the perfect setting for the fictional Penzance Island was found in the leafy, fairy-tale surroundings of Rhode Island.

a waspish candour to Andersonian motherhood. Here was another study of a malfunctioning family unit and the hand-me-down damage parents pass on to their children.

Willis was also a very deliberate choice, but with a side salad of irony. Captain Sharp may live alone in a trailer, a model of inaction, but he is still a cop. 'You can tell when somebody's a cop,' noted Anderson.

'There is something that's often projected from an actual policeman, and Bruce Willis has this cop authority, where even if he's playing something away from what he normally plays, you would never question whether Bruce Willis is the police.'[17] Anderson was calling upon the same sullen grace Willis brought to *Pulp Fiction*.

Murray was full of praise for a superstar a long way from the comforts of Hollywood. 'Life really does change when you go on one of Wes's films – you gotta sit back and relax. But Bruce absolutely delivered. He was really game. It was like, "Let's play."'[18]

Above: Jason Schwartzman takes a cameo role as can-do Khaki Scout Ben – who, while assisting Sam and Suzy's escape, also marries them, though it may not be legally binding. Note the reference to Max Fischer doing Tom Cruise in *Rushmore* in his shades.

Right: Murray and McDormand as the depressed Bishops, whose fraying marriage is a source of Suzy's discontent – a plot line that directly links Suzy with Anderson's childhood woes.

Above: Bruce Willis, a big fan of the director, willingly worked for scale as local police officer Captain Sharp. Anderson loved how Willis brought the baggage of all those starring roles as big screen cops.

Left: A copper-topped Tilda Swinton in a fearsome blue bonnet is known solely as Social Services, the quasi-Victorian representative of authority found in so many children's stories.

Born out of a short-lived venture into scouting as a boy, the Khaki Scouts are among Anderson's greatest comic inventions – and there is a more defined gearshift between comic and tragic in *Moonrise Kingdom*. A wonderful repertoire of incidental sight gags lurk at the back of the frame ... like the two scouts launching a homemade firework (a bottle rocket, perchance?), to land, uncommented upon, behind the main action.

He had lasted no more than a month as a scout. 'I gave it a shot,' he laughed. 'It didn't really take. I never really was much of a camper.'[19] Camping and conformity bring out his allergies. The Khaki troop is another of his societies in miniature, another pack, like the school-body of *Rushmore* or the crew of *The Life Aquatic with Steve Zissou*: a gonzo collective of uniformed boys who chew gum and banter like wiseguy G.I.s from Second World War pictures. They run to military rules, their triangular tents lined up with spirit-level precision, but have the pep and one-liners of television staple *The Phil Silvers Show*.

The 55th Brigade at Camp Ivanhoe is ineffectually governed by the fussbudget Scoutmaster Ward (Edward Norton). Dressed in knee-high socks, shorts, and a butter-yellow scarf, he's a man perpetually surprised at the calamities the universe is willing to spring. 'Jiminy Cricket, he's flown the coop,'[20] he exclaims, informed that Sam has absconded, leaving behind a resignation note written with a note of resignation.

Anderson and Norton had swapped letters for some years, citing a mutual appreciation for one another's work. The only surprise was that it had taken this long for Anderson to find a role for the adventurous star of *Primal Fear* and *Fight Club*. 'He looks like he has been painted by Norman Rockwell,'[21] the director observed appreciatively, noticing an outward innocence.

Norton discerned that his chipper scout leader wasn't so different from Anderson. 'He's a real believer. It was probably the easiest gig I ever had, because all I had to do was turn to Wes and say, "How would you say this line?" Then I would just imitate him.'[22]

The scandal caused by the runaways will travel up the ranks to Fort Lebanon and Commander Pierce (Harvey Keitel with a fulsome Teddy Roosevelt moustache ... or maybe it's Lord Baden-Powell). Here too, Jason Schwartzman takes a bow as a slick scout racketeer in shades, Max Fischer doing his Tom Cruise impression.

For the duration of the shoot, Anderson rented a mansion in Newport, where he stationed his editing room, housed close crew, and hired a great cook. It made everything feel more collegiate, and what Murray called the 'ungodly'[23] hours became less of a burden. Slowly but surely, cast

members began to move in: Murray, Schwartzman, Norton; and pretty soon it became the ultimate expression of a Wes Anderson production under one roof, like a very neat frat house.

Before unloved ones can be retrieved, amends made, and order restored, the storm will finally break, flooding the island, and striking Sam, non-fatally, with a bolt of lightning. The film will swap genres, as Sam and Suzy flee across the church roof through a maelstrom. Anderson set up green screens on location in order to composite-in storm effects, and the film shifts into a quasi-animated mode with forced perspective and miniatures. The blue-black silhouettes of Captain Sharp, Suzy and Sam dangling from a belfry like Hanging Monkeys looked like a page torn from a comic book. Such is a disaster movie as made by Wes Anderson. What he called a 'leap into some sort of magical reality.'[24]

Above: Norton was cast as worrywart Scout Master Ward because Anderson sensed something almost quaint about him. He had what the director thought of as a Norman Rockwell quality.

Below: Suzy and Sam unite across a field in a shot that could define Anderson's use of space, balance, formal camera angles and relative absurdity.

Such was Anderson's reputation and the singleminded bravura of his craft that his new film was given the honour of opening the Cannes Film Festival in May 2012. It was his first invitation to the festival that had nurtured so many of his heroes. Now it conferred on him, too, a similar badge of artistic acceptance. Here, also, was where French reporters taxed him with their intense lines of questioning.

The film proved a (relative) success with $68 million worldwide, but more than that, *Moonrise Kingdom* was hailed as the work of a returning hero. The irony must have pinched. Having been criticized for being too self-involved, too cute, too stuck in his quirky ways, Anderson doubles down on his tics and touches … and the critics go bananas. Perhaps they perceived an added touch of heart – something that has, in fact,

always been a part of Anderson's make-up. Career reappraisals began. The film gained an Academy Award nomination for Best Original Screenplay (his third, following a screenplay nod for *The Royal Tenenbaums* and one for Best Animated Feature Film with *Fantastic Mr. Fox*).

He was now so twee as to be twee proof, said Christopher Orr in *The Atlantic*, describing *Moonrise Kingdom* as 'Anderson's best live-action feature – his best feature, period – since *Rushmore*.'[25]

Interestingly, Philip French in *The Observer* saw this as Anderson's most ambitious work to date. He noticed how the film was, for the first time, evidently about America itself.

Anderson has always protested that he, the filmmaker, does not get to control what his film *means*. 'You don't want to control that side of things,' he said. 'Just let the film live and breathe.'[26]

Focus on characters: how they react, what they might say, how they express what they might need. The meaning will come out of the life of the story. Everyone responds, each in their own way. That's the point – the story intersects with their lives.

And yet, his films contradict their maker. They appear to be entirely the result of specific planning, and he does admit that he likes a script 'locked down'[27] before shooting.

And here, beyond the established kit-bag of Anderson's personal movie hang-ups – parents who don't get their children, children who can't fathom their parents, the bowling ball of divorce, faltering relationships, artistic expression, depression, interior decoration, catching trains: all the *Sturm und Drang* of human (and fox) nature – was politics. Out of his most contained and romantic story sprang the bigger picture.

How so? Well, the Bishops' house is situated on the northern tip of New Penzance in an area significantly named Summer's End. As French intuited, a change is in the salty air. This is not only the end of Sam and Suzy's childhood: a storm is brewing for America. 'Two years have passed since the assassination of Kennedy,' said French, 'the Vietnam war is still largely distant thunder, the phenomenon known as the sixties is starting to rumble on the West Coast, and the country is enjoying its last stage of innocence.'[28]

Anderson agreed: 'It seems like 1965 is really the end of one kind of America.'[29] All those peppy scouts are the foreshadowing of soldiers to come. Asked to give a forecast on what might become of the hopeful couple, left at the end of the movie in the grasp of a relatively happy ending (Captain Sharp takes in Sam, the Bishops try and work things out, Suzy is reading a fantasy, her beloved at his easel), Anderson was realistic. 'These kids that are in the story,' he mused, 'she's bound to end up at Berkeley or something and he's probably going to get sent to Vietnam.'[30]

Was this the sting of maturity critics had been pining for? Surely all of Anderson's films are haunted by death in some shape or form: sharks, tigers, wolves, and now storms.

What lay in store was his most successful, most critically acclaimed, most Oscar-nominated, and most overtly political and deathly film. It was also his most madcap, whimsical, outrageously silly, and precision-built adventure yet. So go figure.

Left: Anderson in his element – by his seventh film, the director had won over critics and audiences, remaining fully committed to his own distinctive style of filmmaking.

THE GRAND BUDAPEST HOTEL

For his ninth film, Wes Anderson went meticulously epic. Here is a period tale within a period tale of legendary concierge Monsieur Gustave H., a rip-snorting adventure bursting at the seams with stolen paintings, lusty dowagers, prison escapes, bobsled chases, and the stirring of fascism

Let's begin with a flashback. When Wes Anderson was a boy, his archaeologist mother would take him and his brothers along on digs. Anderson can remember enjoying a family outing, but the actual archaeology proved deathly dull. Hour upon hour, he would sift though dirt for the odd shard of pottery, which would then be whisked away and labelled by someone more important. However, there was one dig that stayed with him. It was in Galveston, Texas, where, in 1900, a hurricane had buried an entire community in mud. They were excavating a submerged house. Only the top floor showed above ground. Below, the ground floor and basement were perfectly preserved. The entire interior was there, with all its ephemera of life. 'The whole thing,'[1] he marvelled. It was like a lost world waiting to be discovered.

Metaphor alert! Anderson's filmmaking is a form of archaeology – all these perfectly preserved worlds waiting for the light. Which delivers us neatly to the steps of *The Grand Budapest Hotel*, a glorious edifice unearthed from another time, and considered at once to be Anderson's magnum opus ... though historical accuracy was not uppermost in the director's mind.

At this stage of his career, circa 2012, Anderson was held in similar esteem to (and generally lumped in with) such

fellow American auteurs and studio hipsters as Quentin Tarantino, Paul Thomas Anderson, Steven Soderbergh, and David Fincher, though he had more in common with the quirkier end of the spectrum: the Coen brothers, Sofia Coppola, Spike Jonze, and friend and collaborator Noah Baumbach.

In truth, Anderson remained a law unto himself – an island of one in modern Hollywood. 'Eight feature films in, Wes Anderson is basically a genre,'[2] announced Ryan Reed in *Esquire*. Online parodies were proliferating ('*Star*

Above: Ralph Fiennes stars as the impeccable M. Gustave H., concierge of a mythical and fabulous European hotel, man of impeccable taste, and clear cypher for Wes Anderson.

Opposite: Against all preconceptions, the grand farce of *The Grand Budapest Hotel* would break out to become Anderson's biggest hit, the culmination of everything he had done thus far.

Wars if directed by Wes Anderson!'[3])
Saturday Night Live produced a mock
trailer for *The Midnight Coterie of Sinister
Intruders*, a 'tale of handmade horror'[4]
with Edward Norton as Owen Wilson
and Alec Baldwin narrating. 'I'd like to
have a shot at doing the parody myself
and see what I could come up with,'[5]
laughed Anderson, certain he would
make it much scarier. The self-parody
was already built in.

Only in the characteristic creative
thinking of Anderson could a detour
into the life of an august concierge in
a mythical Europe of 1932 become his
first blockbuster.

Our tale begins with the director
browsing at a bookshop in his beloved
Paris. Here he picks up a novel by
the all-but-forgotten Austrian writer
Stefan Zweig. The name rings a distant
bell. Born in 1881, Zweig was a poet,
playwright, novelist, commentator, and
Viennese *bon vivant* who gained great
popularity for the clarity of his prose
and the lavishness of his get-togethers.
Like Anderson, he was a tuning fork
for high culture. He wrote essays on
Dickens, Dante, Rimbaud, Toscanini,
and Joyce. He published a book on
the subject of Marie Antoinette to
whom dowager Madame D.'s tottering
whipped-cream pouf pays tribute. Zweig
was also a bibliophile, who assembled
a famed library in Salzburg. But his life
was edged in tragedy. Having fled the
Nazis – as a lauded Jewish writer, he
was high on their wanted list – Zweig
and his wife took their own lives while
exiled in Brazil in 1942.

Anderson samples a page of Zweig's
Beware of Pity, loves it, and buys the
book. A chain reaction has begun.

Not long afterwards, Anderson read
another Zweig novel, *The Post Office
Girl*, about a lowly clerk summoned
to a distinguished Swiss hotel by her
aunt – who proceeds to reinvent her
charge as a society beauty. One thing

he particularly loved was how Zweig
set up the story 'by having his narrator
meet a mysterious figure who goes
on to tell him the whole novel.'[6]

A few doors down, in another room
in his brain, was an idea he and his
friend Hugo Guinness (artist, scion of
the Guinness clan, and voice of Mr.
Bunce in *Fantastic Mr. Fox*) had been
tossing around for years. In it, the
lead character – name, age, sex and
occupation to be decided – inherits
a big-ticket portrait from an older
admirer, much to the chagrin of said
admirer's relatives.

It was a case of slotting the two
ideas together like pieces of a jigsaw,
and writing the script in collaboration
with Guinness – who was able to
provide a knowledge of the art world
and, as Anderson noted, 'particular
turns of phrase that were not in my
lexicon.'[7] The result was the most
expansive and funny of all Andersonian

Above: Beneath a towering
wig and prosthetics lies Tilda
Swinton as the dowager
Madame D., whose death will
be the catalyst for the ensuing
(and precisely orchestrated)
chaos.

Opposite: The mentor-student
relationship between Gustave
and his lobby boy Zero (Tony
Revolori) stirs into something
deeper and more parental.
For once it is the story of a
good father.

contraptions. Andersonologist Matt Zoller Seitz deemed it 'the culmination of everything he had learned, wedded to a comic velocity we had never seen before.'[8] In other words, while a period piece set in Eastern Europe, it was irrefutably Andersonesque, evoking the lure of such elegant institutions as the Rushmore Academy, the Tenenbaum mansion, and the good ship *Belafonte*. Visually and thematically, *The Grand Budapest Hotel* is the fullest, richest, maddest, and most successful expression of Anderson's gifts.

The eponymous Post Office Girl became quick-witted lobby boy Zero (Tony Revolori), who falls under the tutelage and fatherly spell of the great concierge M. Gustave H. (Ralph Fiennes in career-defining form). Their story unfolds on the snowy flanks of Central Europe. Anderson was seeking an old-world sophistication that was fading as the Second World War mustered on the horizon. The familiar cloud of melancholy hanging over farcical hijinks would turn out to be a storm front.

Europe itself was a big influence on Anderson's thinking. Over the previous two decades, and on numerous train rides, he had got to know the place well – though he willingly admitted that the version of it portrayed in his film owed more to thirties Hollywood. Zubrowka, the name he and Guinness had given to their landlocked domain, chimes with Freedonia from the Marx brothers' *Duck Soup* and all those half-remembered countries made up by Ernst Lubitsch.

The two writers took an extended tour of the continent's remaining gateau-shaped establishments in search of sugary detail. It was the equivalent of the fact-finding mission Anderson undertook for *The Darjeeling Limited*, only with better room service. There was the Hotel Atlantic in Hamburg, dating from 1909 – and the Hotel Imperial in Vienna, built in the 1860s for some unloved duke and duchess who were off soon enough to somewhere more fashionable. The film's fictional beauty spot of Nebelsbad was modelled on picturesque Karlovy Vary in the Czech Republic. Quite literally (West) Bohemian, this spa town hosts an

annual film festival, and boasts the splendid Hotel Bristol Palace with a pink pastel façade, sauna, and nearby funicular railway, from which visiting directors can take in the view. In Prague, they happened upon the Society of Golden Keys, a genuine guild of concierges that discreetly trades contacts and files on its clientele. The organization already seemed like something Anderson might have created – and for the film, it was transformed into the Society of the Cross Keys.

At the hub of the plot is the deluxe hotel of the title, frosted in white and fuchsia, and run to the Swiss clockwork precision of Gustave's unswervable rulebook. His smoothly oiled expertise will be severely tested when the antique Madame D. (Tilda Swinton) – with whom Gustave goes beyond the call of duty – cuts her ties with mortality and leaves the concierge a pricey heirloom (the portrait *Boy with Apple* by made-up

Northern Renaissance master Johannes van Hoytl) ... a move to which a clot of blood relatives don't take too kindly.

While godfathered by Zweig's humanism, critics saw something of the adventures of Hergé's dapper Tintin in the film's headlong plunge out from the hotel into political turmoil (and associated bobsled runs). There is also a sense of moving sideways between scenes as though they're the cells of a comic strip. And reviewers, like trainspotters, began totting up Eurocentric film references: ones to Berlin directors such as Lubitsch, with his sparkling humour; and to Fritz Lang, with his conspiracies. There's a measure of Powell and Pressburger's *The Life and Death of Colonel Blimp* in the way history is delivered like cinematic postcards. And of Billy Wilder, another Berlin exile, whose jokes can cut like a razor blade. Plus – Hitchcock's train movies, odd-man-out 007 adventure *On*

Her Majesty's Secret Service, Ingmar's Bergman's hotel-bound gloom-fest *The Silence*, *Fiddler on the Roof*, and the Overlook Hotel from *The Shining*.

None of which would mean a jot if we didn't have Fiennes there to fast-talk us through the chaos with unsinkable resilience and ingenuity, like a mix of Basil Fawlty and Albert Einstein.

'On a Wes Anderson film, you come knowing what you're in for,'[9] he reported. All the actors were aware they were agreeing to be part of his style. Another brushstroke. Even when depicting high crisis there's an interlacing of voice-over, dialogue, set design, and camera moves like a courtly dance.

Anderson could only shrug. 'When I'm making a film, I'm consciously trying to do something different to what I've done before, but when it's put together, people say they can tell in ten seconds that it's by me.'[10]

Above: Shooting on location in Germany, Anderson sought to take his unique fusion of the real and absurd to new comic heights, but with darker undercurrents than ever before.

Left: The Saxony town of Görlitz provided the perfect picturesque setting, and a hint of the quaint, provincial side of Europe that nonetheless gave itself up to the rise of fascism.

Above: From its lacquered walls to the finery of its costumes (Madame D.'s elaborate coat and dress were modelled on the paintings of Gustav Klimt), the film's design was lavish, bordering on dreamlike.

Opposite: Zero (Revolori) and sweetheart Agatha (Saoirse Ronan). Anderson was hugely impressed with the young actress: she only had a small part, but knew the entire script before walking onto set.

In fact, with his snow-globe vision of Europe between the wars, Anderson was taking his hybrid of the real and absurd to mountainous new heights. For the violent, winter-gripped world outside of the hotel, the director orchestrated a symphony of ski chases, steam-train escapades, mountaintop getaways, jailbreaks … and an establishing shot of the Grand Budapest itself that used miniatures shot against digitally painted backdrops based on the landscapes of Casper David Friedrich. At times, it is almost as two-dimensional as Hergé. And as hyperactive as *Fantastic Mr. Fox*.

They copied Victorian snow portraits – fake backgrounds with fake snow used by well-to-do holidaymakers to photograph fanciful versions of their trips. Anderson told his production department about a scene in the Max Ophüls Zweig adaptation *Letter from an Unknown Woman* in which the lead couple take a fake train ride at an expo with the landscape scrolling past the window. He wanted that feel – reality adjusting to fit both the story and the budget: after all, mounting a 'real' ski chase would have required three weeks of stuntwork in Switzerland.

The result is an Alpine setting as knowingly phoney as the undersea kingdom of *The Life Aquatic with Steve Zissou*.

Inside and out, the asking price was $25 million. While, in the grand scheme of things, this was only half the budget of Bill Murray's oceangoing tragicomedy (let alone the average cookie-cutter Hollywood attraction), getting the money together required an international co-production between Fox Searchlight and the German Federal Film Fund – which made the film half European.

A search began in earnest for a suitable venue for the fictional hotel. There was never a doubt that Anderson was going to shoot in Europe, but it became clear that what he imagined

for the interior of the Grand Budapest in its pomp no longer existed. He had lucked upon a collection of Photocrom pictures (essentially colourized black-and-whites) in the Library of Congress, offering views of European grandeur from the turn of the century. They were ghost visions of a world wiped from the map. 'It's like Google Earth access to the turn of the century,'[11] he said, attaching copies to each of the scripts he sent out to his cast. A mood was set.

To find a hotel grand enough was a forlorn hope, but Anderson's good fortune held. In the Saxony town of Görlitz, they discovered a cavernous former department store that had miraculously escaped being bombed in the Second World War. The *Görlitzer Warenhaus* formed a tidy rectangle around a stained glass Art Deco atrium, and offered the perfect architecture on which production designer Adam Stockhausen could assemble the flush

of scarlet velvet, patterned carpets, and brass trimmings of the Grand Budapest. 'It had beautiful bones,'[12] said producer Jeremy Dawson. The parking lot doubled for the entrance.

'It's much bigger than anything we could have built, and it's grander, and it's kind of real,'[13] said Anderson, who would have moved in if the rooms weren't sets. The motif of buildings subdivided into boxes, and boxes within boxes, permeates the entire film, from hotel to mansion to prison to train carriage.

In every frame, the accumulation of detail is extraordinary, even by Anderson's standards. More than ever, the warp and weft of the decor shed light on character, extended jokes, and built up layers of illusion, mystery and meta-commentary. 'I feel like the dialogue and the writing ends up being not entirely naturalistic, not by my choice particularly,' said Anderson, straining

to make sense of his holistic impulse. 'Somehow, I feel like it needs its own world to exist in.'[14]

Here are some brief examples: the name of Gustave's scent, *L'Air de Panache*, serves as metaphor and gag for both Fiennes's performance and Anderson's method. This was spraying on the aroma of panache over reality. Zero's great love, Agatha (Saoirse Ronan), has a birthmark the shape of Mexico on the side of her face (a telling asymmetry). Why Mexico? We are never told, but can we infer a link to the location of communist outcast Trotsky's exile and murder? Agatha works at famed Nebelsbad bakery Mendl's, assisting in the creation of the exquisite and pivotal *Courtesan au Chocolat* (a bespoke smothering of profiteroles provided by a local Görlitz baker) – basically Gustave in cake form. Confectionery becomes a prevailing symbol for an era: delicate, refined, wonderful to the taste, useful for concealing illicit items, and gone too quickly.

Painting-cum-MacGuffin, *Boy with Apple*, was provided by English artist Michael Jackson with the same mix of Bronzino and Hans Holbein that had been applied to the look of *Rushmore*. All the artwork is significant. On the walls of the older Author's drab sixties study, we catch sight of a study in woolly mammoths, emblems of extinction.

Designed by Milena Canonero, the costumes took a similarly multifarious approach. The uniforms of Gustave and Zero came in a cartoonishly non-classical purple to chime with what Anderson deemed the musical colours of the 1932 floor of the film. Whereas the black leather coat worn by lugubrious, motorbike-riding henchman Jopling (Willem Dafoe), his teeth filed to vampiric points and so uncivilized he *doesn't* have a moustache, was an exaggeration of

Left: The prison gang begin their elaborate escape. To get into character, Harvey Keitel (second from the left as jailbird Ludwig) encouraged his fellow inmates to spend forty-eight hours living on the prison set, during which time they devised an entire history for their characters.

Below: Willem Dafoe as the dastardly, quasi-vampiric hitman Jopling. His costume and BMW motorcycle were directly inspired by leather-clad Nazi-era dispatch riders. His teeth were modelled on *Nosferatu*.

a thirties-era dispatch rider coat and made by Prada. While Madame D.'s tomato-red silk coat and dress were inspired by the art of Gustav Klimt.

The score by Alexandre Desplat, featuring excerpts from Russian folk tunes, included (on special request from Anderson), the shivery, *Doctor Zhivago*-like notes of a balalaika as the musical voice of the film.

Equally, the narrative structure of *The Grand Budapest Hotel* takes Anderson's Russian Doll approach to dizzying new levels. Of course, he and Zweig share a predilection for framing their narratives with active storytellers. It is a way of setting a mood, or as Anderson dubbed it, 'encroaching on a story by stealth.'[15] But here he assembles four tiers of story, each nested in the next like an archaeological dig. As secrets are unveiled, we leap back in time. It's as if a microscope is being brought into focus from the

present to 1985 to 1962 to 1932, where
the great story of M. Gustave is to be
found. It is also like the unwrapping
of a marvellous confectionery.

At the outermost layer of this
elaborate narrative confection, we meet
a young girl, clad in a beret like an
Eastern European version of book-mad
Suzy Bishop from *Moonrise Kingdom*.
She is visiting a chilly cemetery with
a well-thumbed copy of a book called,
yes, *The Grand Budapest Hotel* – clearly
a favourite. The film exists within those
pages just as *The Royal Tenenbaums*
spills out of its own book.

A bronze bust of the Author (we
learn no more of his given designation)
is located in that very cemetery.
Cue: flashback. The Author represents
Zweig himself. First as an older man,
played by Tom Wilkinson, recording his
views to camera in 1985 (recalling the
documentary framework of *Moonrise
Kingdom*), dispensing views on the
border country that lies between fact
and fiction, memoir and novel. Lines
are lifted directly from Zweig. The
Author's recollections then plunge
us back to what Anderson called the
'theoretically fictionalized'[16] younger
Author, played by Jude Law, in 1962.
He pays a visit to a Grand Budapest
Hotel left to decline beneath the yoke
of communism. Here the older Zero
(F. Murray Abraham) will recollect his
life with M. Gustave. Cue: flashback.

Effectively, the film has two
narrators, one lurking within the other's
narration. It's also worth noting that
both older and younger versions of the
Author wear cuts of the brown Norfolk
Tweed suits and tan shirts favoured by
the director (authors within authors!)
Meanwhile, each period comes with an
era-specific aspect ratio (films within
films!) For the modern scenes, including
1985, it is the contemporary widescreen
of 1.85:1. For the 1962 era, with the
Grand Budapest a ghost ship smeared

in green and orange, the epic 2.35:1
Cinemascope ratio was used. Back in
1932, it is the old, near-square Academy
ratio of 1.37:1, for which Anderson shot
with antique anamorphic lenses that
went misty at the edges.

M. Gustave, said Anderson, was
also 'modelled significantly on Zweig.'[17]
Fiennes sports the same neat moustache
and slicked-back hair. Anderson fretted
that he 'had never written about
someone who is not an American hero
before.'[18] It didn't matter: Gustave still
possessed many traits of the director's
leading men – culture, self-regard,
dress sense, a capacity for scrapes, and
the ability to deliver a cuss word like a
cymbal crash.

To play his hero, viewed forever
through the adoring memories of his
former lobby boy, Anderson had one
face in mind. He had enjoyed Fiennes'
lunatic rages in *In Bruges*. Elsewhere,
there was some fine comic timing in

his work – as well as the irony that he'd
famously filled the jackboots of a Nazi
in Steven Spielberg's *Schindler's List*. 'I
met him maybe ten years ago when I
was at somebody's house and went into
the kitchen and he was sitting there,' he
recalled. 'I wanted to find something to
do with him. He's intense.'[19]

Fiennes, he knew, could handle
the long speeches. He was Method,
but politely so, in the Russian way. 'He
wants to do it from the inside out,'[20]
appreciated Anderson. The fastidious
Fiennes imagined a history for the
character we never learn of on screen,
where he remains an enigma. How
Gustave arose from a poor background
in England, working his way up from
the 'lowest of the low'[21] at some grand
hotel, doing favours for the clientele,
storing up secrets. Then crisscrossing
Europe, lobby to shining lobby, a
life sequestered at the gilt-edge of a
forgotten age.

The Oscar-wining English actor (another scion of a distinguished dynasty – explorer Sir Ranulph Fiennes is his uncle) grasped that performance in Anderson's films was as defined as the wallpaper. 'Wes has a strong sense of how the lines should be, and he is often leading you toward that,' he accepted, adding that when it came to setting a tone for how to play Gustave they settled on somewhere in the middle of 'high camp, hyper, sort of crazy, or very naturalistically.'[22]

Yet again, we can draw parallels between a punctilious hero and the neatnik guile of Anderson. They both (very politely) seek complete control over their plush worlds. But Fiennes is a comic wonder in his own right, mixing the remorseless slapstick of Jacques Tati with Cary Grant holding onto to his dignity beneath Hitchcock's abuses, and a touch of Murray's ineffable narcissism, though not quite the drooping spirit.

'From the start, his Gustave – suave, austere, sometimes frazzled – seizes the comic and emotional centre,' wrote Richard Corliss in *Time*, effusive in his praise. 'A brilliant, troubled man in a preposterous, essential job, he sees his mission as making people happy, and he does so with an efficiency that raises craft to art. So does Wes Anderson.'[23]

For his underling, protégé, confidant, partner-in-crime, and surrogate son Zero (named for the Broadway star Zero Mostel, and to suggest a blank slate onto which Gustave can compose a person), Anderson foresaw a stateless refugee of Middle Eastern origin. 'I don't know if he's an Arab or a Jew, or a mixture of them,'[24] he said. There is no direct mention of the Holocaust, but it seeps from the film's pores. The subtle inference that Zero might have Jewish blood, as his dubious papers are constantly being inspected by the fascist ZigZag authorities (Anderson's

Above: Owen Wilson as the concierge M. Chuck, who replaces Gustave after the ZigZag party takes over the country. Note the fine view of the elaborate lobby, built onto the shell of an old department store.

Left: Another regular, Edward Norton, appears as Inspector Henckels, finicky representative of the new fascistic regime. Referencing the Holocaust within what is ostensibly a comedy involved a fine balancing act.

Oppostie: Gustave (Fiennes) and Zero (Tony Revolori) surreptitiously hit the hotel safe. The affectionate central mentorship between concierge and lobby boy would be one of the film's key charms.

alt-universe take on the Nazis), triggers a deliberate real-world undercurrent.

The film is lit up by this central relationship between the hyper-verbal ringleader and his faithful sidekick – a customary Anderson double act that harks all the way back to Dignan and Anthony in *Bottle Rocket*. However, though Zero's life is often threatened – it was the era for such things – Gustave offers a rare example of devoted fatherhood.

In search of the right look, Anderson had casting directors at work across Israel, Beirut, and Morocco, only for Zero to walk through the door in Anaheim in California. Revolori had never acted professionally before, but sent in an audition tape. Anderson liked his innocence, and decided to stick with American accents from American stars. It gave the feel of a movie from the thirties or forties ... Hollywood abroad.

Over a dozen name-parts populate the ensuing cocktail of farce and high adventure, which boils down to Gustave being framed for murdering Madame D., absconding with the painting, hiding the painting, getting arrested, and escaping from prison (all with the invaluable assistance of Zero) – and evading the dastardly Jopling and the ZigZag brigades. The chocolate box of new and regular stars willing to take small but memorable roles was a gauge of what it meant to enlist in an Anderson film in 2012. Aside from those already mentioned, there was Jeff Goldblum, Edward Norton, Adrien Brody, Harvey Keitel, Léa Seydoux, Bob Balaban, Owen Wilson, Jason Schwartzman, and Murray (of course).

For the duration of the shoot, from January to March 2013, they all stayed in the same hotel in Görlitz. 'We had a cook I know from Italy who cooked for us and we had dinner together every night of the movie,' said Anderson. 'Almost every night was a little buzzing dinner party.'[25]

RALPH FIENNES

M. Gustave

F. MURRAY ABRAHAM

Mr. Moustafa

MATHIEU AMALRIC

Serge

ADRIEN BRODY

Dmitri

WILLEM DAFOE

Jopling

BILL MURRAY

M. Ivan

THE
GRAND
BUDAPEST
HOTEL

Directed by WES ANDERSON

SAOIRSE RONAN

Agatha

JASON SCHWARTZMAN

M. Jean

LÉA SEYDOUX

Clotilde

TILDA SWINTON

Madame D.

TOM WILKINSON

Author

FOX SEARCHLIGHT PICTURES in Association with INDIAN PAINTBRUSH and STUDIO BABELSBERG Present an AMERICAN EMPIRICAL PICTURE
Costume Designer MILENA CANONERO Original Music by ALEXANDRE DESPLAT Music Supervisor RANDALL POSTER Editor BARNEY PILLING
Co-Producer JANE FRAZER Executive Producers MOLLY COOPER CHARLIE WOEBCKEN CHRISTOPH FISSER HENNING MOLFENTER Produced by WES AN
Screenplay by WES ANDERSON GRANDBUDAPESTHOTEL.COM

JEFF GOLDBLUM

Kovacs

HARVEY KEITEL

Ludwig

JUDE LAW

Young Writer

EDWARD NORTON

Henckels

OWEN WILSON

M. Chuck

introducing
TONY REVOLORI

Zero

Above: Past perfect — in February 2014, Anderson wraps up for the New York premiere of *The Grand Budapest Hotel.* The daring and splendid film was to become his biggest success.

Left: As part of the film's elaborate (and successful) marketing campaign, good use was made of the sheer volume of Anderson regulars and newcomers who populate the film. It also offers a helpful tally of facial hair.

BUDAPEST HOTEL" U.S. Casting by **DOUGLAS AIBEL** U.K. Casting by **JINA JAY**
signer **ADAM STOCKHAUSEN** Director of Photography **ROBERT YEOMAN, A.S.C.**
T **RUDIN STEVEN RALES JEREMY DAWSON** Story by **WES ANDERSON & HUGO GUINNESS**
ES **ANDERSON**

PERFECTLY FORMED

The best of Wes Anderson's short films and commercials

IKEA – 'Unböring' (2002): A touch looser in style, this commercial is still a magnificently Anderson-esque idea. A family are seen bickering amid the tidy proportions of a living room, only for the camera to reveal – surprise! – they are on the shop floor of an IKEA store.

American Express – 'My Life. My Card.' (2006): A stroke of pure Anderson in-joke ingenuity, this commercial for the famous credit card does not simply parody an Anderson film (starring regulars Jason Schwartzman and Waris Ahluwalia, dressed solely in white, out front of a stylish mansion) – it parodies the making of an Anderson film, with the director brusquely walking us through his daily on-set rigmarole of dealing with the various demands of his querulous crew. He is wearing a tan safari suit.

Hotel Chevalier (2007): From the miniature black-and-white original of *Bottle Rocket* onwards, Anderson's shorts and commercials – all made in his inimitable style – extend his universe and the reach of his humour. Indeed, this dalliance in a Parisian hotel room actively functions as a prologue to *The Darjeeling Limited*.

SoftBank – 'Mr Hulot' (2008): An all-too-brief one-take riff on slapstick marvel Jacques Tati's *Mr. Hulot's Holiday* – with Brad Pitt, no less, wearing a canary yellow hat, shirt and pants.

Stella Artois – 'Mon Amour' (2010): A dashing young man brings his date back to his hi-tech Parisian apartment. Well, hi-tech in that classic Andersonian gadget-filled sixties-take-on-the-future way (it's like a swish rendition of the *Belafonte* in *The Life Aquatic with Steve Zissou*). While he gets into something more stylish, she foolishly dabbles with the control panel, launching a frenzy of hidden functions before being swallowed by the pea-green sofa. Not to worry, she has activated the automated pouring of Stella.

Prada – 'Castello Cavalcanti' (2013): Set precisely in September 1955 during a motor race through the titular and timeless small Italian town, this beautiful near-eight-minute wonder has Jason Schwartzman's fast-talking American driver crash out and decide to stay. It also advertises Prada, if you care to notice.

Prada – 'Candy' (2013): A collaboration between Anderson and Roman Coppola, this love triangle set across three sleek Parisian episodes finds regular Léa Seydoux unable to make her mind up between two ridiculously handsome suitors and best friends – Peter Gadiot and Rodolphe Pauly made up to look uncannily like one another.

H&M – 'Come Together' (2016): While ostensibly advertising the clothing store, this is in fact a charming reboot of Anderson's 'train of thought' sequence from *The Darjeeling Limited*. Adrien Brody is the conductor spreading Christmas cheer onboard his delayed train (gilded in pastel green) while the camera moves laterally and vertically between compartments and their lonely passengers. To date, Anderson's only Christmas movie.

Right: Jack Whitman (Jason Schwartzman) and his unnamed, unreliable girlfriend (Natalie Portman) gaze out from their Paris room in miniature marvel *Hotel Chevalier*.

The Grand Budapest Hotel took its bow at the Berlin Film Festival on 6 February 2014. Where else could be more appropriate? A model of the titular establishment adorned the lobby of Berlin's famous Hotel Adlon (a hotel within a hotel!) The reviews hailed old tricks delivered with a new confidence. But no one suspected such a dare would finally find Anderson such a large and appreciative audience. The film made a startling $173 million worldwide, nearly three times that of *Moonrise Kingdom* and *The Royal Tenenbaums*. The momentum carried it all the way to the Academy Awards, a year hence, with nine nominations, including Best Picture, Best Director, and Best Original Screenplay. It would win four: Production Design, Costume Design, Make-up and Hairstyling, and Best Score.

To this day, it remains the film viewed as the high-water mark of the Andersonesque, but not everyone was in agreement. In the *New Republic*, David Thomson called it a 'ferment of decoration.'[26] There were ructions in certain corners about appropriating the horrors of the twentieth century for a knockabout comedy. But such a view misses the crucial point – it is the audacious disparity between the comic mode and the underlying seriousness that makes the film quietly devastating. As Anderson said, 'There's something heavy that's there that I was aware of, and I've never had a movie where there's this much blood.'[27] The loss of childhood has become the loss of an entire civilization.

Brimming with a nostalgia for a world that never quite was, it is a film about the nature of storytelling. And with Robert Yeoman's cinematography zipping along corridors and up in funiculars, it never lets us forget the mechanics of that telling. The film brings into focus Anderson's wider thematic concerns. What are stories for? What do they do? Why do we need

them so much? Can they actually heal? By spinning illusion from truth, comedy from grief, Anderson's storytellers are mastering death.

'The great wager that Anderson makes and wins in *The Grand Budapest Hotel*,' deduced Jonathan Romney in *Film Comment*, 'is that a piece of film art can be extremely refined, artificed, and calibrated virtually to the point of being mechanical – yet can still accommodate emotional content, even if that content communicates itself on a rather indirect, rarefied level.'[28]

On a second or third viewing, the comedy recedes and that underlying tragedy catches the breath. In small, almost throwaway, yet dagger-sharp lines (still veiled in humour), the older Zero alludes to the fate of his loved ones. He mentions that Agatha and his infant son were taken by the 'Prussian Grippe.'[29] As for the heroic, unstinting, marvellous M. Gustave: 'In the end, they shot him.'[30]

Above: Framed framing – emphasizing the irony that Gustave (Fiennes), keeper of the Grand Budapest Hotel's keys, will find himself locked up.

ISLE OF DOGS

For his ninth film, Wes Anderson returned to the rigours of stop-motion animation. What better medium for a science fiction stray dog story that also serves as a political satire while paying homage to the breadth of Japanese culture?

Given the collection of made-to-measure fables that represented Anderson's career to date, no one was expecting controversy to rear its ugly head. But here it was. Anderson's latest film, *Isle of Dogs*, another two-year odyssey of painstaking stop-motion animation shot at 3 Mills Studios in London, but situated plot-wise in a Japan twenty years into the future, arrived to accusations of a Western artist superimposing his droll agenda on another culture. Appropriation alert!

Written with his *Darjeeling Limited* companions Jason Schwartzman and Roman Coppola, the story begins with the machinations of an evil mayor, Kobayashi, who even at puppet dimensions is the spitting image of Japanese superstar Toshiro Mifune. Due to complex historical issues concerning rival dog- and cat-worshipping clans (summarized in a mystical prologue), the wicked Kobayashi has exiled the dog population of made-up metropolis Megasaki City to the nearby Trash Island on the basis of a confected triple threat of canine overpopulation, dog flu and snout fever. First to be dumped, by cable car (in a left-to-right dolly shot), is Spots (Liev Schreiber), formerly bodyguard and companion to Kobayashi's orphaned twelve-year-old ward Atari (Koyu Rankin).

A distraught Atari will commandeer a small plane, crash-land on Trash Island, and track down his beloved dog. In his quest, he will be assisted by a pack of chatterbox ex-pets, and a problem stray named Chief (Bryan Cranston), whose bite is worse than his bark.

None of which exactly screams any great offence against political correctness. Unless, that is, you're a cat lover.

The journey the dogs and their boy undertake across the post-apocalyptic zones of Trash Island is

Above: Shaggy-dog storytellers – Wes Anderson reuniting with his *Darjeeling Limited* partners Roman Coppola and Jason Schwartzman.

Opposite: *Isle of Dogs* was intended as an affectionate, in-depth homage to Japan and its culture, but its heightened comic tone would lead to accusations of cultural appropriation.

syncopated with chapter headings, flashbacks, newsreels, montages, and subplots – with Greta Gerwig as busybody Max Fischer-like American exchange student Tracy Walker stirring classmates into pro-dog insurrection against Kobayashi and his cat-loving minions. These also include the epidemic of cover-ups by his totalitarian regime.

Featuring robot dogs, computer terminals, Atari dressed in a David-Bowie-esque silver jumpsuit and space helmet, as well as a general aura of neon-smudged dystopian Anime and video-game level-hopping, this comes under the heading of Wes Anderson's First Science Fiction Film. But it leans backwards in time, mixing ancient samurai movie iconography and the clunky, sixties doodads of his previous films.

'This is definitely a reimagining of Japan through my experience of Japanese cinema,'[1] reported Anderson.

But times had changed. Debate raged as to whether it was appropriate for Anderson to take his pick from Japanese culture like a salad bar. In short, who gets to make what art?

Think pieces were thought. Noses stuck into the air, critical teeth gnashed, attention-grabbing headlines put on page, and diatribes dashed off on social media. 'Wes Anderson's *Isle of Dogs* is wading into a world that didn't exist when he started making his stop-motion fable,'[2] noted Marc Bernadin in the *Hollywood Reporter*. Anderson treats Japanese culture like wallpaper, he proposed, rather than an essential part of the drama. But pull at that thread, he conceded, and modern culture might quickly unravel.

Steve Rose in *The Guardian* rang plenty of alarm bells. Why are all the dogs voiced by white, American

actors? Isn't Gerwig's blonde and freckled Tracy classifiable as a 'white saviour'[3]? He compared *Isle of Dogs* to recent whitewashed offenders like *Ghost in the Shell* and *Doctor Strange*. 'When there's an explosion at one point,' he remonstrated, 'it's a mushroom cloud – a reminder that Japan suffered a nuclear attack, from a filmmaker from the country that attacked them? Really?'[4]

There is a chill that comes with the echo of Hiroshima and Nagasaki in Trash Island. But then, as with the shadows of the Holocaust in *The Grand Budapest Hotel*, that chill is a daring fissure to reality within the storytelling.

Having bestowed (mostly) lavish praise upon his previous film, it was clearly time for critics to topple Anderson from his pedestal. Commentators were back-pedalling through his work and finding a

Opposite: Well groomed – the Isle of Dogs team formally photographed at the Berlin Film Festival. Top row: Mari Natsuki, Jason Schwartzman, Tilda Swinton, Wes Anderson, Jeff Goldblum, and Roman Coppola. Seated: Akira Takayama, Bill Murray, Kunichi Nomura, Bryan Cranston, Koyu Rankin, Liev Schreiber, Greta Gerwig, Yojiro Noda, and Bob Balaban.

Right: Puppet master – Anderson poses with his model cast at 3 Mills Studios in London.

pattern. Look how he turned India into a tourist trap for *The Darjeeling Limited*, they cried, missing the point that it was a country viewed through the eyes of a trio of outsiders. What's with all the jokes about fascism and suicide and divorce?

In hindsight, it is perhaps unfortunate that while the English-speaking dogs are rounded, sympathetic characters, the Japanese humans remain, shall we say, enigmatic. You can argue that Anderson is so locked up in the ivory tower of his ideas that he has become deaf to potential insensitivity.

But surely Anderson is exploring concepts of language, communication, and the universality of storytelling. At its outermost layer, the film is wryly structured as an introduction to Japanese culture to a Western watcher, with Courtney B. Vance as Anderson's omnipresent 'voice of the movie.'[5]

Yet the director also insisted that conversational Japanese should speak for itself without subtitles. 'You don't necessarily know what people are saying a certain amount of the time, but you sort of get it.'[6] The film is an entirely different experience if you are a native Japanese speaker.

During the writing, Anderson added a significant fourth musketeer in Kunichi Nomura, an interior designer, magazine editor, and translator for American movies. He had worked on Sofia Coppola's *Lost in Translation*, and she made the introductions. Nomura went bar-hopping with Anderson on his first trip to Japan. They quickly became friends, and he would bring a native eye to the story and play the villainous Mayor Kobayashi.

One level further in, with a typically brilliant flourish of Andersonian whimsy, at crucial,

dramatic moments we get Frances McDormand's Interpreter Nelson packaging Kobayashi's pronouncements into pithy news bulletins, Tracy's helpful pep talks, and the responses of a lumpy, electronic Simul-Translate device. Also, to be clear, the pooches don't speak English; their barks have been translated for our convenience.

There are so many finely wired ironies at work in *Isle of Dogs* that the critics' case against Anderson was far from cut and dried. For one thing, postwar Japanese culture was already heavily influenced by America. Appropriations lie within appropriations! And for another, people were getting awfully worked up over a shaggy-dog story.

Which is a good point. How did Anderson even come up with this cockamamie tale of tails? What were the co-ordinates of the *Isle of Dogs*?

You could say it began with a road sign. Anderson was in London for *Fantastic Mr. Fox*. On his way to 3 Mills Studios near Stratford, he spied a sign to the Isle of Dogs, a clutter of former docks and warehouses turned residential zone that jutted out into the Thames. The name struck him as endearing. What if there was literally an island populated by dogs alone? He filed it away for future use. After all, Anderson liked islands (though, strictly speaking, London's Isle of Dogs is a peninsula). *Moonrise Kingdom* and *The Royal Tenenbaums* are each set entirely on an island – the latter being Manhattan. This time it was an island off the coast of an island.

You could say it began with dogs. Anderson was setting things right by canines. When *Moonrise Kingdom* came out, *The New Yorker* voiced concern that the director had it in for our four-legged friends. More controversy! In that film,

wirehair fox terrier Snoopy, faithful mascot for the 55th division of Khaki Scouts, ends up slain with an arrow to the neck. In *The Royal Tenenbaums*, the family beagle Buckley gets run over by Owen Wilson. In *The Life Aquatic with Steve Zissou*, the nameless three-legged dog gets marooned on the pirate island (an isle of dog). And in *Fantastic Mr. Fox*, the guard dog Spitz, another beagle, is fed spiked blueberries. This amounted to serial pooch abuse. The author of the *New Yorker* piece, Ian Crouch, cited such dog frailty as 'examples of the slightly anti-social lack of sentimentality that runs through all of Anderson's work.'[7]

Finally, in *Isle of Dogs*, the creatures would serve as heroes (say it slowly and the title is a pun). But only after being exiled, drugged, starved, losing limbs, eyes, ears and teeth, and narrowly avoiding incineration.

Below: Every frame in Anderson's ersatz Japan speaks to the intricacy of his design. Note not only the classic Andersonian symmetry (centred on Bill Murray's pooch Boss), but the echo between costumes and crockery, with its zigzag hints of television transmissions, and the chopsticks repeating the aerial.

Opposite below: Pack mentality – for Anderson the idea of having dogs as protagonists was about playing to the movie tradition of the faithful companion. In life, he remains largely ambivalent about pets.

The writers displayed contrasting levels of devotion to pets. Schwartzman, noted Anderson, 'has a dog who he's lived with for eleven years or so and he's one hundred percent a dog person.'[8] Coppola had a cat that he loved. Anderson himself had neither. His partner Juman Malouf kept a couple of goats at her place in Kent in England, but he wouldn't call himself a goat person. Still, when he was twelve, the family pet was a Black Labrador called – you got it – Chief. 'I don't think he had the same complexity,' he reflected. 'He was pretty straightforward.'[9]

Dogs, for Anderson, were more of a movie thing. He was interested in the emotive power of the boy-and-his-dog genre: tearjerkers like *The Adventures of Rin Tin Tin*, *Lassie Come Home*, and *Old Yeller*; adventure movies like *Call of the Wild* and *White Fang*. There are reminders, too, of Tintin and his faithful wire fox terrier Snowy. On a darker thread, Anderson drew upon the child-traumatizing, anthropomorphic novels (and adaptations) of Richard Adams like *Watership Down* and *The Plague Dogs*; the latter story is about two dogs that escape from a medical research facility, and may be carrying bubonic plague. In *Isle of Dogs*, we will meet a pack of outlaw dogs bearing scars from medical research.

'The truth is, I like dogs as characters in movies,'[10] he said, and, of course, his dogs really function as people – a pack of alphas as dysfunctional as the Tenenbaums.

You could say it began with Japan. Anderson had been thinking about Japanese cinema since he began bingeing on Akira Kurosawa movies at university. Up until then, he had only seen *Rashōmon*, a Samurai-slanted dissection of memory and murder. Once he got to grips with Kurosawa's phenomenal career – not only the great *jidaigeki* period dramas like *Seven Samurai* and *Yojimbo*, but his noirs, gangster flicks, and family dramas – he knew he loved Kurosawa. It was the same absorption in an artist and culture he had felt with Satyajit Ray and India. Or Federico Fellini and Italy. He loved how these countries revered their filmmakers.

But the Japanese references stretch far beyond Kurosawa. There are homages to the likes of Yasujirō Ozu, *Godzilla* creator Ishirō Honda (and associated *kaiju* monster movies), celebrated animator Hayao Miyazaki, the many realms of Manga, and medieval Yamato-e woodblock art and the Edo-era Ukiyo-e landscape prints of Utagawa Hiroshige. The entire story is borne along by the martial beat of Taiko drums on the soundtrack.

Right: Akira Kurosawa's masterpiece *Seven Samurai* was a foremost object of adoration and homage. Second from the left is Kurosawa's star and muse Toshiro Mifune, who would be the basis for the Mayor Kobayashi puppet.

When it came to a montage depicting the preparation of poisoned sushi, Anderson demanded that the puppet chef's skills be depicted with unerring accuracy. Otherwise it would look silly. It took six months to create less than a minute of action.

However you wish to read the finished film, Anderson had gone into the project with a scholarly degree of immersion in an entire culture.

Indeed, it was his first exposure to the country, thirteen years before he came to write the movie, which settled the matter. 'It wasn't just that I had a great visit here,' he explained, 'but I really felt inspired by being in Japan. I felt like I wanted to make something.'[11]

His flight from America had reached its zenith, though this would be a dream Japan made in miniature in East London. Filmmaking has expanded his life experience. What he likes so much about living in Paris is that it feels like he is living in a movie set. For *Isle of Dogs*, he spent six years thinking about Japan every single day. 'It really changes you, and I like the idea of being changed in that way.'[12]

You could say it was about getting back on that stop-motion horse. He loved the format ... the complete creative control he gained over the material ... the fact that everything had to be made from scratch. He could build an entire world in miniature, and *Isle of Dogs* encompassed a far larger geographical paw-print than *Fantastic Mr. Fox*.

This was a story, he emphasized, that was suited to animation. 'It would be much more difficult to make this story in live-action, but we could.' He pictured Kurosawa making it as a live-action movie, and he could see how good it might be. But the reasons not to were compelling: 'If you're going to have talking dogs,' he admitted, 'it's not so bad if they're puppets.'[13]

Interestingly, Anderson pointed out that his abiding love of stop motion began with the Rankin/Bass holiday specials like *Rudolph the Red-Nosed Reindeer* and *The Life and Adventures of Santa Claus*, which he saw as a boy. These quintessentially American productions were actually animated in Japan. As Taylor Ramos and Tony Zhou put it in their introduction to the *Isle of Dogs* edition of the *Wes Anderson*

Collection, Anderson 'has closed the loop on one of his own key influences.'[14]

He still found the process of bringing puppets made of metal and foam and fabric to life a mysterious one. That rippling side effect of animating fur (here sourced from alpacas) he had kept in *Fantastic Mr. Fox* now had a term: *boiling*. It was an error caused by fine hairs moving under hot lights between frames. The result was like an injection of real life into the hermetic world of his miniature universe.

You could say the new film was a result of everything that's been described here. In the afterglow of *The Grand Budapest Hotel*'s success, Fox Searchlight readily backed their favourite son's new venture (budgets remain elusive) and the film began inching its way into being at 3 Mills Studios from October 2016.

'I think I've definitely reached the point where I accept that this is sort of who I am,'[15] said Anderson philosophically. The camera was moving at right angles. References were being spread like confetti. The mood was deadpan. Bill Murray was chilling in the recording studio. Call it instinct.

Top: Even among the sci-fi trappings of a Japan seen in the near future, Anderson could not resist his bibliographic urge to depict the pleasures of a library.

Above: For all the accusations of cultural appropriation, Anderson was also reflecting how Japan had already usurped Western cultural icons such as baseball.

Still, *Isle of Dogs* posed a thrilling new problem: how do you have twenty-five visually interesting areas on a garbage dump? Anderson's answer was simple: 'All garbage is super-organized.'[16] There would be carefully compartmentalized zones of refuse, some of it compacted into symmetrical, aluminium cubes similar to Pixar's *WALL·E*, and we are provided a series of overhead maps to get a handle on things geographically.

Why garbage? Obviously, there was the metaphor for these discarded dogs, but really it was just another childhood thing. 'I loved Oscar the Grouch on *Sesame Street*,' said Anderson. 'I loved this TV show they had in America called *Fat Albert* where they had a clubhouse on a garbage dump.'[17] After years of refinery and good taste, trash was the signature motif. His films have so often been accused of cluttering, so why not make a film out of clutter? More than that, for Anderson junkyards represent

imaginative spaces in which a world can be reconstituted from old parts, which is a thinly veiled allusion to his own *modus operandi*.

'It's an inspired molecular universe created by an immensely visionary and technologically crack team,'[18] boasted Tilda Swinton, returning in the part of a bug-eyed pug called Oracle who can see into the future (basically because she is able to decipher television weather reports).

Each zone is coded by colour and variety of junk. For a soot-black backdrop there are piles of car batteries and old cathode ray tubes. A beautiful hovel is constructed from tiny, individually coloured glass sake bottles. Over one hundred 1950s sake bottle labels were created from scratch.

As the heroes travel across the twelve sets representing the split personality of the island, it evolves into the ruins of a lost civilization. There is a rusted

Above: While crossing the many video-game-like zones of Trash Island, Chief (Cranston) and the boy Atari (Rankin) pass through an area made up of surreal sculptures of discarded plumbing.

Opposite: Wide-eyed Pug Oracle (Swinton) has the uncanny ability to decipher television weather reports into 'dog', thus predicting the future. Swinton actually recorded her few lines while on vacation with the director.

power station, a ruined golf course, and a derelict theme park – Kobayashi Park – based on Nara Dreamland, once considered Japan's answer to Disneyland, but abandoned once the postwar boom faded. It was like civilization left for dead after a *Godzilla* movie, or *The Grand Budapest Hotel* faded into obscurity.

For the expressionist sprawl of Megasaki City, production designer Paul Herrod drew on Japanese metabolist (organic) architecture, the dream reality of mega-metropolis Tokyo, and, squeezed in between, the folksy Japanese home-life of Kurosawa and Ozu's urban movies. There were more wheels within wheels – Kobayashi's Brick Mansion is based on the old Imperial Hotel in Tokyo, which was designed by Frank Lloyd Wright, a modernist *American* architect. Elsewhere we get the retro-futurist chic of production design legend Ken Adam's *Doctor Strangelove* and 007-goes-to-Japan extravaganza *You Only Live Twice*.

Gazing at the wonder of the director's habitual comic confectionery, *The Guardian*'s Peter Bradshaw wondered why it was only now, with Japan, that progressive opinion should be nettled. 'Anderson is arguably no more or less insensitive or chauvinist here than in his treatment of central European culture in *The Grand Budapest Hotel* or indeed dear old Blighty in *Fantastic Mr. Fox*.'[19]

As a whole, the frenetic *Isle of Dogs* may not be Anderson's most emotionally telling work – it is closest in tone to the oddball epic of *The Life Aquatic with Steve Zissou* – but nevertheless it is a jewellery box of sublime touches.

A brief explanation of animatics: from *Fantastic Mr. Fox* onwards, Anderson has relied upon these moving blueprints. In rudimentary terms, they are animated storyboards, created on a computer as a 'movie before the movie.'[20] They give a director a sense

of how his film will flow. In Anderson's case, this includes all the proposed framing, camera moves, and an idea of the sound design. Using Anderson's stage-one stick-figure storyboards (on the usual mix of hotel stationery and ripped-out notebook pages) as the template, his in-house animatics have a goofy Hanna-Barbera aesthetic that could grace a stand-alone animated movie.

On the flip side, the tool has allowed the director to choreograph ever more elaborate and hilarious set pieces, but something of the naturalistic ease of his early films has been lost. Anderson himself estimated that as much as ninety percent of *The Grand Budapest Hotel* was rendered as an animatic before a frame was shot in earnest.

The sheer volume of set piece, story, location, and character here outdid *Fantastic Mr. Fox*. Anderson warned his team this one was going to be 'puppet-heavy.'[21] In total 2,200 puppets populate 240 sets built across 44 stages. The sheer invention is stunning, and slightly unhinged.

Unlike the Foxes (family and species) of *Fantastic Mr. Fox*, who lean toward being humans in fur, the dogs of *Isle of Dogs* still have the physical mannerisms of their kind. No animal is caught wearing a suit; they run, walk, scratch, snarl, pivot hind legs, and reflexively sit with an uncanny affinity to the real thing. The animators were encouraged to bring their pets to work: the dogs would wander about, sniff one another's butts, sleep, and generally bug people, unaware they were the stars of the show.

Nevertheless, all the dogs talk like Wes Anderson characters. 'Stop licking your wounds!'[22] barks Chief at a fellow mutt doing just that. When we first relocate to Trash Island, there is a terrific pause before Rex, despite having blond fur and a white snout, delivers a very human expression (kind of doggy despondency) and launches into Edward Norton's anxious patter. They also come with customary Andersonian hang-ups.

The joke is that they are a pack of alpha dogs with alpha names: Norton's Rex, a finicky former indoor dog; King

(Bob Balaban), a sacked spokes-dog for a brand of discontinued dog food; Duke (Jeff Goldblum), an inveterate gossip; Boss (Murray), the onetime mascot for a high-school baseball team who still wears the jersey; and Cranston's outlier Chief, who is fully undomesticated. Chief has the wild side of Mr. Fox or Steve Zissou: the type that would literally bite the hand feeding him. Though Rex tends to be the organizer of this bunch of equal-status alpha dogs (he's a four-legged Francis Whitman or Scout Leader Ward), every decision has to be put to a vote.

A second, subtler joke is that these self-involved hounds are now masterless. They are like the warriors of *Seven Samurai*, a gang of furball *rōnin* left to wander the land in search of purpose. There are shots against a wheat field – so desaturated it looks black and white – that are a direct lift from Kurosawa's masterpiece ... though with dogs, not samurai.

They are mostly of indeterminate breed (we don't get Latin derivations as we did with the critters of *Fantastic*

Mr. Fox), with heart-shaped noses and mangy coats. Halfway through, the jet-black Chief is subjected to a bath and comes out a piebald black and white, which might be the most profound character transformation in any Anderson movie.

For each human puppet, animators chose from a readymade set of emotional expressions like paints in a paint box – a dozen different mouth shapes to be switched in and out.

With more puppets came more stars. Anderson's ensembles (his packs) were growing exponentially, but they were of familiar breeds. There were welcome additions in Gerwig, Cranston, Schreiber, Nomura, ten-year old Canadian-Japanese debutant Rankin (who served as model for his Atari puppet), and ex-Beatle wife Yoko Ono as a forlorn scientist.

Anderson claims that he doesn't go through agents, but calls direct. By now many of these actors were his friends. Even for those he didn't know well, he'd track down a number: 'Hi, it's Wes Anderson, I have a movie ... '[23]

They'd rarely say no. Gerwig he had got to know through her partner Noah Baumbach; Cranston didn't need to see a script.

There is a tangential in-joke in the casting of both Murray and Scarlett Johansson among the dogs. The latter plays Nutmeg, a pretty former show-dog falling into a tentative *Lady and the Tramp* romance with Chief. Of course, Murray and Johansson starred in Japan-set quasi-romantic hit *Lost in Translation*. Which likewise danced along the line of cultural appropriation. Indeed, Sofia Coppola based her film on a commercial her father had shot starring Kurosawa, advertising the same (real) Suntory whisky that Murray's lonely actor had come to Tokyo to promote.

Francis Coppola, with friend George Lucas (whose *Star Wars* helped kick-start Anderson's whole thing with movies), gave financial backing to the ageing Kurosawa's later films. And hadn't Kurosawa openly appropriated the storylines of Westerns and pulp thrillers for his Samurai classics to begin with?

Left: Among the ruins of a former theme park, Atari (Rankin) finds he is not tall enough to ride. Note the pastiche of 19th century woodblock artist Toyohara Kunichika in the cut out samurai.

Opposite: Nuclear sunset – a boy on his dog scans for signs of life, silhouetted in a serene wide shot undercut with a strange orange gleam that hints at Japan's jolted history.

身長制限 (You must be this tall)

市の最善のために

YASHI

あなたの投票をお願いします
[For the Greater Good of Megasaki City]

Left: Interpreter Nelson (Frances McDormand) gives an update following Mayor Kobayashi's news conference. Note the reference to *Citizen Kane* in the huge mural of the politician's face.

Above: Mayor Kobayashi (Nomura) takes a bathtime conference with Professor Watanabe (Akira Ito) and assistant-scientist Yoko-ono (Yoko Ono). Note the pastiche of classical Yamato-e landscape art in the tile mosaic.

THE FOUNDING FATHERS

A checklist of the key influences on the Wes Anderson style

François Truffaut: The wizard of the French New Wave has been a guiding light – especially his depictions of spirited but sensitive youth. Anderson's discovery of Truffaut's debut *The 400 Blows* in a Houston video store changed his life. Here was a filmmaker making vibrant use of his own life.

Martin Scorsese: The American great who championed a young Anderson. He offered up highly personal, character-driven stories set in stylized, genre-bound worlds.

Hal Ashby: Seventies Hollywood purveyor of deadpan humour in such films as *The Last Detail, Harold and Maude, Shampoo,* and *Being There.*

Satyajit Ray: Indian humanist giant under whose spell *The Darjeeling Limited* was made, but whose tender influence can be felt throughout Andersonland.

Louis Malle: Another versatile French director whose coming-of-age tale with a streak of incest, *Murmur of the Heart,* has been of particular importance. He also made a series of documentaries on India, and worked with Jacques Cousteau.

Orson Welles: Primarily for the formalism of *Citizen Kane* and the housebound family saga of *The Magnificent Ambersons.*

Akira Kurosawa: *Isle of Dogs* is virtually a tribute to the Japanese master, albeit with stop-motion dogs. And don't discount the fixed viewpoints and softly-spoken family dramas of Yasujirō Ozu.

Ernst Lubitsch: Famous Berlin-born director turned Hollywood exile who cultivated a deceptively meaningful brand of comic whimsy. During the shoot of *The Grand Budapest Hotel,* Anderson provided a library of relevant titles for his actors, including Lubitsch's satire on fascism and fame *To Be or Not To Be,* and his cynical tale of love and deception *The Shop Around the Corner.* Frustratingly for the eager players, Anderson only provided one copy of each.

Heat: Yes indeed, Michael Mann's mid-nineties crime classic is repeatedly referenced across Anderson's work – most noticeably in *Rushmore,* with its thing for macho crime films. Anderson loves how few critics notice.

J.D. Salinger: Less for the reclusive author's teen-despondency classic *Catcher in the Rye* than his Glass family saga, which served as a primary source.

Hergé: Legendary Belgian cartoonist (real name: Georges Prosper Remi) behind the adventures of Tintin, legendary man-boy reporter-sleuth of defined apparel and emotionally wayward friends.

Charles M. Schulz: Legendary American cartoonist behind the world of *Peanuts,* whose sad-sack depictions of life's iniquities through the medium of kids struck a particular chord with Anderson.

Left: The young, daringly brilliant Orson Welles in *Citizen Kane.* The great actor and filmmaker has been a seminal influence on Wes Anderson.

The New Yorker: For the critical views of Pauline Kael; for its trim intellectual take on New York and, if there's room, the world; for its wit and sagacity, droll cartoons, and highfalutin book reviews. *The French Dispatch* is Anderson's tribute to a lifelong love of the weekly magazine.

Hullabaloo aside, the reviews were generally upbeat. The film cracked the ninety percent approval rating on the *Rotten Tomatoes* review aggregator site – a clumsy but influential tally of a film's critical reception. By comparison, *The Life Aquatic with Steve Zissou* languished at fifty-six percent, not including recent reappraisals.

The box office results were decent, though $64 million worldwide suggested that Anderson was back preaching to the converted.

With *Isle of Dogs*, there is an unshakeable sensation that Anderson's visual brilliance is running on a treadmill. All the referencing is borderline ritualistic. You feel the lack of tangible actors – that sublime tension in Anderson's best work between the geometric rigours of the design and the impulsiveness of his heroes. Once the story whittles down to Chief's redemption it loses its quirky momentum.

Yet those repositories of emotion are still here. As ever, it's a funny-sad movie about family, friendship, growing up, and the things that finally define you. Death lingers over the fun like a cotton-wool cloud. As Sophie Monks Kaufman says in her study on Anderson, 'he uses death as a way to embellish characters.'[24] Atari has lost both his parents to a train crash (he's another orphan). Spots and then Chief become surrogate fathers.

What is conspicuous is that the film is more overtly political, with Megasaki City descending into stage-managed political hysteria. The fever of allusions is not yet done, you can add to the Petri dish of Anderson's multiverse John Frankenheimer's paranoid trilogy of political thrillers: *The Manchurian Candidate*, *Seven Days in May*, and *Seconds*. From the manipulations of Kobayashi to Rex tiresomely putting every group decision to a vote,

Anderson is considering the nature of democracy. A pack mentality isn't always ideal. Moreover, the real world is making itself heard.

During the early stages of production, Donald Trump came to power in the USA, and their portrayal of government-sanctioned deportation looked startlingly prescient. 'The world changed a lot while we were making it,' admitted Anderson. 'We often thought what's happening around us was related to what's happening in the story.'[25] He found he was making a politically relevant talking dog movie. Fur real.

Above: Stop-emotion – Chief becomes mentor and father figure to Atari in much the same way as Zissou with Ned (in *The Life Aquatic with Steve Zissou*) and Gustave with Zero (in *The Grand Budapest Hotel*).

THE FRENCH DISPATCH

For his tenth film, Wes Anderson concocted a multi-tiered love song to journalism. Set in a fictional French city across the fifties, sixties and seventies, it centres on the exploits of a weekly magazine run by a band of expatriate American intellectuals

As *Isle of Dogs* reached cinemas in the spring of 2018, whatever misgivings had surrounded his latest film, Wes Anderson was now classified as filmmaker, artist, brand, and cultural icon, even if such terms were liable to make him squirm. Fans had become followers. He was the head of the world's most orderly cult. At 48 years old, his suits were finely tailored and his apartments elegantly furnished, but he was still rake-thin and boyish. Outwardly, he was an unlikely doyen, but he had become influential. Beyond his own output (which offered a level of consistency few could match), he had produced *The Squid and the Whale* for friend and collaborator Noah Baumbach in 2014. Testament to how far Anderson had risen, in the same year he also produced *She's Funny That Way*, the first film in thirteen years by seventies humanist Peter Bogdanovich, a director whose work he had revered in his college days.

Online especially, he was subject to adoration, analysis, and homage (as well as its evil twin parody). He was someone to be collected and collated. Critics (there was a growing band of specialists like Matt Zoller Seitz) spoke of him like a family member or therapist. 'I don't know Wes Anderson personally,' admitted Sophie Monks Kaufman in her intensely personal evaluation of his work, *Close-ups – Wes Anderson*. But, she went on to say, 'I do know that, at some point in his life, his understanding of sadness connected with my understanding of sadness.'[1]

An entire community now existed devoted to the point of obsession with his piquant, abstract, enclosed worlds of eye-popping colour, inhabited by eccentric yet melancholic heroes who somehow reflected our own, unglued lives. Anderson and his films bring people together.

Take Wally Koval, who grew up in Delaware before moving to Brooklyn, a travel enthusiast and Anderson die-hard. What he particularly loved was how his favourite director evoked emotion from location, and had made pilgrimages to Paris, Budapest, and India. Everywhere Koval went he took pictures of sights that reminded him of Anderson's movies – the colour schemes, the symmetry, the signature motifs – and posted them on his Instagram account *Accidentally Wes Anderson*. He soon began to add shots submitted by other photographers: hotel exteriors, train carriages, cable cars, theatres, lighthouses, libraries, and telephone booths. They came from as far afield as Antarctica and Uruguay, each carrying something intangibly Anderson about them. 'It's that wildcard attribute that is difficult to put your finger on,' said Koval. 'But, simply put, you know it when you see it.'[2] That Instagram account now has nearly one million followers.

Above: Wes Anderson at 48, looking as if he's hardly aged a day, but now a highly respected figure within the film industry, and one of very few men who can pull off plaid with herringbone.

Opposite: The cartoon-themed poster for *The French Dispatch* – revealing not only the extravagant cast list but also plot points – blends a classic *New Yorker* cover from 1 June 1946 (yes, that specifically) and the poster for Jacques Tati's *Mon Oncle* (1958), with a hint of Tintin covers thrown in for good measure.

Anderson didn't dare stop to register such idolization, or, God forbid, quantify his own value as a filmmaker. Otherwise he just might grind to a halt. It was vital to preserve that wildcard attribute that would surely wither with self-analysis. As ever, he was intent on his next film. Which was to be a return to the relief of live action, he was willing to admit that much. But what form it would take had yet to emerge. In interview, he had mused airily about something Dickensian: 'Every Dickens story has been done so many times there's really no room [for another]. But I think I would love to do a story that was set in Dickensian London – somewhere around the Strand.'[3]

Gathering dust in the back of a drawer was the script for *The Rosenthaler Suite*, written during the long shoot for *Fantastic Mr. Fox*. Commissioned by producer Brian Grazer (who tended toward middlebrow Hollywood hits like *Apollo 13* and *A Beautiful Mind*), it was a reworking of 2006 French comedy *My Best Friend*

(Mon meilleur ami) about an obnoxious antique dealer challenged by his business partner to bring forth the best friend he often mentions. She rightly believes the friend is made up. With a valuable vase at stake, the dealer cajoles a chatty cab driver into posing as his fabricated buddy. In Anderson's take, the setting moves from Paris to New York, and centres on an art dealer, with a collection of paintings by the artist Moses Rosenthaler the prize in question. There was talk of George Clooney and Anjelica Huston as the now rival art dealers, and Adrien Brody as a Polish cab driver. However, asked about the film in 2010, Anderson denied that he was ever going to direct it, suggesting Roman Coppola was a more likely candidate. 'I was just hired to write,' he shrugged. '...But in the end I liked a lot of it very much.'[4]

Eight years later, *The Rosenthaler Suite* hadn't entirely been forgotten, but Anderson was not headed to London or New York, but somewhere typically unusual and closer to home.

Above left: The final edition of *The French Dispatch* on sale in the fictional French city of Ennui-sur-Blasé (in reality the picturesque Angoulême).

Above: The offices of *The French Dispatch*, whose delivery van is in Zissou-blue. The Dachshund is another reference to *Mon Oncle*. The filmmakers added shop fronts, street signs and different skylines to what they'd shot on location.

It began with talk that Anderson was planning a musical. Commentators were united in their approval – what better genre for a master of artifice and musical montage? Moreover, it was to be his first film set in his beloved home from home, France, in the unmoored years following the Second World War. Tilda Swinton was mentioned as a possible star. These rumours turned out to be mostly bunkum. Where they were spot-on was about the location (and, roughly speaking, the era): Anderson would be shooting his new film in Angoulême, the 'balcony'[5] of the southwest, a picturesque hilltop city boasting perfectly preserved medieval ramparts, greenery, and a charming Old Town quarter. It was the French equivalent of an Anderson set. However, Angoulême would not be playing Angoulême.

When the six-month shoot began in November 2018, producer Jeremy Dawson set the record straight. This was not to be a musical at all, but another unconventional ensemble piece of no fixed genre, though certainly funny. The film's lavish cast was to feature regulars like Owen Wilson, Frances McDormand, the aforementioned Swinton, and (shock!) Bill Murray, but there were intriguing newcomers in the mix like Benicio del Toro, Elisabeth Moss, and Timothée Chalamet. The subject would be a magazine run by an expatriate American from a made-up French metropolis going by the distinctly Andersonian name of Ennui-sur-Blasé (roughly speaking Boredom-on-Apathy (which serves as a fair description of Bill Murray's house style), and catering for an American readership. To give film and magazine their full, unexpurgated title, this is *The French Dispatch of the Liberty, Kansas Evening Sun.*

The project was backed by Anderson's regular partners at Fox Searchlight, though having been green-lighted for a relatively compact $25 million (a similar price to *The Grand Budapest Hotel*), parent studio 20th Century Fox was subsequently sold to Disney. Which effectively brought Anderson back into the fold of the studio that had once funded *Rushmore*, *The Royal Tenenbaums*, and the profligate

Left: Bill Murray as Arthur Howitzer, the magazine's stalwart editor and anchor for the film's multi-part structure. While modelled on real-life editors and journalists, there is no missing an element of Anderson, the director, in the character.

Opposite: Howitzer discusses the forthcoming issue with the waiter from the nearby Café le Sans Blague. Note the labels pertaining to the writers of film's three main stories – Roebuck Wright (Jeffrey Wright), Berensen (Tilda Swinton) and, hidden behind the waiter, Krementz (Frances McDormand) – plus Sazerac (Owen Wilson). The board is essentially a map of the film.

voyage of *The Life Aquatic with Steve Zissou*. There were no hard feelings – Anderson looked like good business these days.

In summary, it was another reasonably priced wildcard production that juxtaposed American savvy with European flare, and more than a waft of self-portraiture. 'The story is not easy to explain,' Anderson sheepishly admitted to French publication *Charente Libre* midway through filming (a point when he craves secrecy). "[It's about an] American journalist based in France [who] creates his magazine. It is more a portrait of this man, of this journalist who fights to write what he wants to write. It's not a movie about freedom of the press, but when you talk about reporters you also talk about what's going on in the real world.'[6]

By now, you will know that throughout his career Anderson has shown an appreciation for the fourth estate. In *Rushmore*, Max Fischer was the proud publisher of school newspaper the *Yankee Review*. At the heart of *The Life Aquatic with Steve Zissou* lies the profile Cate Blanchett's intrepid reporter is attempting to elicit from Murray's titular oceanographer. Look closely and you'll see that the newspaper stories glimpsed in *The Grand Budapest Hotel* are nearly all written out in full.

You will also be aware that Anderson possesses a religious devotion to esteemed American weekly *The New Yorker*, whose sardonic touch and intellectual rigour have not only been a guiding light in his life, but can be felt in the fabric of his filmmaking. Specifically in the case of *The Royal Tenenbaums*, but Anderson's entire sensibility and that of the neatnik cultural bible are closely aligned. He possesses bound volumes of it dating back to the forties.

Fittingly, therefore, it was *The New Yorker* that got the exclusive revealing that Anderson's love of the magazine, right down to specific writers and individual stories from its long history, was the direct inspiration behind his new film. Conceived alongside the latest line-up of familiar collaborators in Roman Coppola, Hugo Guinness, and Jason Schwartzman – though the screenplay is credited solely to Anderson

– this was the closest he had ever come to channeling actual events.

The structure is an anthology movie of sorts, with three separate stories (or articles) linked together by a framing mechanism set in the offices of *The French Dispatch* where the final issue is being assembled: the three articles have been selected for republication on this momentous occasion. Here, amid the jazzy clutter of the old-school publishing business (the issue notes are pinned to a cork board beneath the rubric 'Level of Completion' like a list of shots in an edit suite), editor Arthur Howitzer (Murray, naturally) holds court. Books and back issues line the walls, and three Bakelite telephones lurk on the editor's orderly desk. Anjelica Huston provides the observational voice-over. We are in a French outpost of what is still very much Andersonland.

Sagging at the edges, Howitzer is a stew of *The New Yorker's* founding editor Harold Ross (former stringer for the *Salt Lake Telegram* turned member of New York's elite Algonquin Round Table, and celebrated in equal parts for his pranks, temper, profanity, and perfectionism – so Murray to a tee) and reporter-at-large A.J. Liebling (the boulevardier writer from Manhattan with a nose for a 'mountebank'[7] who had sojourned in Paris during the Second World War and spun silken sentences out of pop cultural minutiae). Howitzer gets waiter service direct to his desk from the local Café le Sans Blague, which translates to the Café of No Joke. Among his devoted if nonchalant team – another haphazard family – is Herbsaint Sazerac (Wilson in a telltale beret), a twist on Joseph Mitchell, famed portraitist of New York life.

Each of the three stories within the story features their respective author as narrator (essentially reading their piece aloud) and their own pastiche on a *New Yorker* headline, before flashing back to take up the events it portrays.

Concrete Masterpiece, by J.K.L. Berenson (a coppery Swinton), profiles an art dealer and his obsession with obtaining the work of del Toro's inmate-artist. This segment is based on a six-part profile of the British dealer Lord Duveen written by S.N. Behrman in 1951, but a fair amount of fiction has gone into the mixing bowl.

From *Fantastic Mr. Fox* to *Moonrise Kingdom*, painters and paintings are recurrent motifs; in *The Grand Budapest Hotel*, the hotly contested masterpiece *Boy with Apple* serves as the MacGuffin. Providing insight into how Anderson often slides ideas between films, del Toro's enigmatic artist is named, yes, Moses Rosenthaler, and he has painted a series of pictures based on his muse – beautiful prison guard Simone (Léa Seydoux). By the way, the art dealer in question, Julian Cadazio, is played by Adrien Brody.

Revisions to a Manifesto has Frances McDormand as political journalist Lucinda Krementz getting to the nub of the student revolution of the late sixties, with Chalamet as a skinny radical with voluminous hair and a cigarette perched provocatively at the corner of his mouth

at all times. He is named Zeffirelli, presumably in tribute to Italian director Franco Zeffirelli. The roots of this segment lie in a two-part article on the Paris uprising of 1968 written by Mavis Gallant.

The third of these 'features within the feature', *The Private Dining Room of the Police Commissioner*, is a food piece, or starts out that way. Prized food writer Roebuck Wright (based partly on author James Baldwin and played by Jeffrey Wright) is the scribe of this exploration of police cookery that boils over into crime and the kidnap of the son of Mathieu Amalric's police commissioner, with Saoirse Ronan on hand as a corrupt floozy.

Above: A staff meeting at *The French Dispatch*. Left to right: Elisabeth Moss, Wilson's Sazerac (in a beret), Swinton's Berensen, legal advisor Fisher Stevens and story editor Griffin Dunne.

Visually – much like the instantly identifiable layout of *The New Yorker* – Anderson showed no signs of changing his ways. Rather, he was elaborating on them. Interspersed among the usual colourful palate (yellows and tobacco browns for office life, brighter hues for the cut and thrust of reportage) is Anderson's first use of black and white since the original *Bottle Rocket* short. The smooth geometry of camera movement even took to occasionally cutting corners and actually circling events. Sticking with the trick used to delineate period on *The Grand Budapest Hotel*, each era comes with its own aspect ratio.

Given this was a romanticized take on French life, inspiration was drawn from some of the greats of French cinema, included in an extensive library of DVDs, books and articles made available to the cast to maximize assimilation into the Gallic vibe.

Returning cinematographer Robert Yeoman cited a quintet of films he and his director soaked up beforehand to get the 'feeling of the French movies of the period, both thematically and stylistically.'[8] These were Jean-Luc Godard's episodic New Wave drama *Vivre Sa Vie*; Henri-Georges Clouzot's brilliant nerve-jangler *Diabolique*; the same director's murder mystery *Quai des Orfèvres* (Amalric mentioned that his character was based on Louis Jouvet's inspector); Max Ophüls's tri-part exploration of pleasure, *Le Plaisir*; and that foundation stone of the Anderson style, François Truffaut's New Wave classic *The 400 Blows*. Each of the three stories within the film, said Yeoman, held their own 'creative possibilities.'[9]

Exterior shooting took place in the quaint and mercifully quiet environs of Angoulême. But beautiful as they were, they were insufficiently corny – Anderson wanted to layer up clichés like a mille-feuille, and aestheticized the streets with the addition of shop fronts, street signs,

and silhouettes of gothic towers. He even changed the seasons, layering the sidewalks and cobbles with fake snow. In terms of physical scale, it was his biggest production yet. With four different story elements crossing multiple timelines, over 125 individual sets were built. For interiors, a derelict felt factory on the edge of town became the perfect ersatz movie studio, with three main stages, workshops, storerooms, and carpentry mill.

Above: Anderson rediscovers black and white. Incarcerated artist Moses Rosenthaler (Benicio Del Toro) is guarded by Simone (Léa Seydoux).

Top: An expectant in-crowd in a classic Anderson set-up, featuring art collector Julian Cadazio (Adrien Brody) and other key cast members.

For the sequence set inside a prison that houses del Toro's painter, they relocated to another former factory where the structure suggested rows of cellblocks (and one execution chamber). They transformed the proposed look of their prison accordingly. 'We were talking about the Orson Welles film *The Trial*,' said production designer Adam Stockhausen, 'where all the sets were built inside this train station and you can kind of see off the edges of the sets and see the architecture of the train station beyond it.'[10] Like the empty Görlitz department store that became the Grand Budapest Hotel, the 'overarching sense of the place'[11] was poking through into the film's tongue-in-cheek universe.

French comedy giant Jacques Tati's extravagant production *Mon Oncle* – portraying a whimsical collision between tradition and modernism in postwar France – was another spiritual touchstone. Of course, Tati's indefatigable slapstick can be felt in Murray's many misfits as well as Ralph Fiennes' exertions as M. Gustave in *The Grand Budapest Hotel*. For *Mon Oncle* he had built entire city streets in a studio

near Nice, a set that enshrined a fairy-tale France of tight, cluttered streets and shuttered windows. One further inspiration, reported Stockhausen, was Albert Lamorisse's *The Red Balloon*, which mixed a 'beautifully grimy city'[12] with glorious colours 'that come popping out from that.'[13]

It was a busier shoot than ever. Actors came and went, with the vast supporting cast stretching out to encompass forty different named parts, and succinct but memorable roles for the likes of Edward Norton, Willem Dafoe, Christoph Waltz, Fisher Stevens, Liev Screiber, Lyna Khoudri, and Jason Schwartzman as *Dispatch* cartoonist Hermes Jones. As they completed their days or weeks on the film, departing cast members dropped hints that this was the most challenging Anderson adventure they had ever worked on. While there was the usual, eloquent script, he encouraged improvisation in every scene. Not that there was any loss of *esprit de corps* among the extended family of cast and crew. They were housed at the beautiful Le Saint Gelais hotel in the centre of town, where Anderson hosted nightly gatherings.

To keep the mood classy, he would always dress for dinner.

'We stay together under one roof, we eat together as a family, we travel together as the members of an explorers' club,' rejoiced Swinton of life on the good ship Anderson. 'Our journeys together become the films, and vice versa. The feeling is of shared playtime – serious playtime, but always with a twinkle in its eye and towards a bright horizon.'[14]

For Bill Murray, less his muse than his spirit animal, working with Anderson is almost a chemical process: you just have to relax, be part of it, like a flower in a still life.

'We are promised very long hours and low wages,' he sighed, deadpan to the last. 'And stale bread. That's pretty much it. It's this crazy thing where you're asked to come and work a lot, and you lose money on the job, because you wind up spending more in tips than you ever earn. But you get to see the world, and see Wes live this wonderful, magical life, where his dreamscape comes true. So, if we show up, he gets to have all his fun, and I guess it's because we like him that we go along with this.'[15]

Left: Getting into the revolutionary spirit – McDormand's Krementz (centre) joins students Juliette (Lyna Khoudri) and Zeffirelli (Timothée Chalamet) on the front lines.

As this book wends its way to the printers, *The French Dispatch* awaits release, with the anticipation reaching frenzy among fans. Websites bided their time, picking apart the helter-skelter trailers for clues.

Even compared to *The Grand Budapest Hotel* – tonally, perhaps, the closest relative – this is clearly going to be Anderson's most densely packed and structurally complex film. And likewise, *The French Dispatch* is attempting to synthesize recent European history, and something of its own times, as order duels with chaos in the guise of riots (on the streets and in the prison), chases and shoot-outs. But it is also another dissertation on the mysteries of the creative process – art, writing, cookery, political manifestos – and on those who interpret the value of the world. In this, maybe there is a joke here at the expense of all those journalists who attempt to decipher the mind of the director.

The French Dispatch marks the continued work of arguably the most distinctive director at work today – and one not likely to convert those that can't stomach his made-to-measure whimsy. A single frozen frame would tell you it belongs to the vision of Wesley Wales Anderson, and all the delightful contradictions that come with him.

That he is such an individualist, an auteur (if you go by the French theory). But that he's also a devoted collaborator, nourished by the community of his films. Each film is a reunion. 'Wes is a pack animal,'[16] quipped Roman Coppola. The family keeps expanding. He portrays the world with the affectedness of a toy theatre, yet there are few filmmakers able to hone in on such human truths. On first viewing, his films are extremely funny – and on the second, heartbreaking. He has cultivated his own corner of the Hollywood system, at the service of nothing but his own whims, but it is a space fertilized by the full pantheon of cinema from Satyagit Ray to Michael Mann.

How was it M. Gustave H. was so beautifully described in *The Grand Budapest Hotel*? Ah yes: 'His world had vanished long before he ever entered it, but he certainly sustained the illusion with a remarkable grace.'[17]

That's Anderson – sustaining the illusion with remarkable grace.

SOURCES

INTRODUCTION

1. *Rushmore* screenplay, Wes Anderson and Owen Wilson, Faber & Faber, 1999
2. *Bottle Rocket* Blu-ray, Criterion Collection, 4 December 2017
3. *Close-ups: Wes Anderson*, Sophie Monks Kaufman, William Collins, 2018
4. *NPR.org*, Terry Gross, 29 May 2012
5. *GQ*, Chris Heath, 28 October 2014
6. Ibid.
7. *GQ*, Anna Peele, 22 March 2018
8. *The Guardian*, Suzie Mackenzie, 12 February 2005
9. *The Royal Tenenbaums* screenplay (introduction), Wes Anderson and Owen Wilson, Faber & Faber, 2001
10. *The Grand Budapest Hotel* screenplay, Wes Anderson, Faber & Faber, 2014

BOTTLE ROCKET

1. *NPR.org*, Terry Gross, 29 May 2012
2. Ibid.
3. *The Wes Anderson Collection*, Matt Zoller Seitz, Abrams, 2013
4. *The Telegraph*, Robbie Collin, 19 February 2014
5. Ibid.
6. *NPR.org*, Terry Gross, 29 May 2012
7. *Icon*, Edward Appleby, September/October 1998
8. Ibid.
9. *Rushmore press kit*, Touchstone Pictures, October 1998
10. *Icon*, Philip Zabriskie, September/October 1998
11. *Interview*, Arnaud Desplechin, 26 October 2009
12. *Los Angeles Magazine*, Amy Wallace, December 2001
13. Ibid.
14. *Live from the New York Public Library: Wes Anderson (via Nypl.org)*, Paul Holdengräber, 27 February 2014
15. *The Wes Anderson Collection*, Matt Zoller Seitz, Abrams, 2013
16. *Vulture*, Matt Zoller Seitz, 23 October 2013
17. *Icon*, Philip Zabriskie, September/October 1998
18. *Los Angeles Magazine*, Amy Wallace, December 2001
19. *Live from the New York Public Library: Wes Anderson (via Nypl.org)*, Paul Holdengräber, 27 February 2014
20. *Texas Monthly*, Pamela Colloff, May 1998
21. *The Wes Anderson Collection*, Matt Zoller Seitz, Abrams, 2013
22. Ibid.
23. *Premiere*, October 1998
24. *Icon*, Philip Zabriskie, September/October 1998
25. *Texas Monthly*, Pamela Colloff, May 1998
26. *Rushmore* screenplay (foreword), Wes Anderson and Owen Wilson, Faber & Faber, 1998
27. *The Wes Anderson Collection*, Matt Zoller Seitz, Abrams, 2013
28. Ibid.
29. *FlickeringMyth.com*, Rachel Kaines, 11 January 2018
30. *Premiere*, October 1998
31. Ibid.
32. Ibid.
33. *The Making of Bottle Rocket*, Criterion Collection Blu-ray, 2017
34. Ibid.
35 *Los Angeles Times*, Kenneth Turan, 21 February 1996
36. *The Washington Post*, Deeson Howe, 21 February 1996
37. *D Magazine*, Matt Zoller Seitz, February 2016
38. *Esquire*, Martin Scorsese, 1 March 2000 (posted)

RUSHMORE

1. *The Wes Anderson Collection*, Matt Zoller Seitz, Abrams, 2013
2. Ibid.
3. *Icon*, Philip Zabriskie, September/October 1998
4. *The Wes Anderson Collection*, Matt Zoller Seitz, Abrams, 2013
5. *Rushmore* screenplay, Wes Anderson and Owen Wilson, Faber & Faber, 1999
6. *The Wes Anderson Collection*, Matt Zoller Seitz, Abrams, 2013
7. Ibid.
8. *Dazed and Confused*, Trey Taylor, 2 June 2015
9. *Salon.com*, Chris Lee, 21 January 1999
10. Ibid.
11. *Newsweek*, Jeff Giles, 7 December 1998
12. *Sunday Today*, Willie Geist, 15 April 2018
13. *Nobody's Fool*, Anthony Lane, Vintage, 2003
14. *The Wes Anderson Collection*, Matt Zoller Seitz, Abrams, 2013
15. *Charlie Rose*, 29 January 1999
16. *Rushmore press kit*, Touchstone Pictures, October 1998
17. *The Wes Anderson Collection*, Matt Zoller Seitz, Abrams, 2013
18. *Rushmore press kit*, Touchstone Pictures, October 1998
19. Ibid.
20. *The Wes Anderson Collection*, Matt Zoller Seitz, Abrams, 2013
21. Ibid.
22. *Rushmore press kit*, Touchstone Pictures, October 1998
23. *The Wes Anderson Collection*, Matt Zoller Seitz, Abrams, 2013
24. *Rolling Stone*, James Rocchi, 11 March 2014
25. *Close-ups: Wes Anderson*, Sophie Monks Kaufman, William Collins, 2018
26. *Rushmore* screenplay (introduction), Wes Anderson and Owen Wilson, Faber & Faber, 1999

27. Ibid.
28. Ibid.
29. Ibid.
30. *The Royal Tenenbaums* screenplay, Wes Anderson and Own Wilson, Faber & Faber, 2001
31. *The Life Aquatic with Steve Zissou* screenplay, Wes Anderson and Noah Baumbach, Touchstone Pictures, 2004

THE ROYAL TENENBAUMS

1. *The Wes Anderson Collection*, Matt Zoller Seitz, Abrams, 2013
2. Ibid.
3. *The Royal Tenenbaums* press kit, Touchstone Pictures, 2001
4. *The Wes Anderson Collection*, Matt Zoller Seitz, Abrams, 2013
5. *The Royal Tenenbaums* press kit, Touchstone Pictures, 2001
6. Ibid.
7. *The Wes Anderson Collection*, Matt Zoller Seitz, Abrams, 2013
8. *The Royal Tenenbaums* press kit, Touchstone Pictures, 2001
9. *The Wes Anderson Collection*, Matt Zoller Seitz, Abrams, 2013
10. *Rebels on the Backlot*, Sharon Waxman, William Morrow, 2005
11. Ibid.
12. *The Royal Tenenbaums* international press conference, 2 September 2002
13. *The Royal Tenenbaums* press kit, Touchstone Pictures, 2001
14. *The Royal Tenenbaums* international press conference, 3 September 2002
15. *The Royal Tenenbaums* press kit, Touchstone Pictures, 2001
16. Ibid.
17. Ibid.
18. *The Royal Tenenbaums* international press conference, 3 September 2002
19. *The Wes Anderson Collection*, Matt Zoller Seitz, Abrams, 2013
20. *The Royal Tenenbaums* international press conference, 3 September 2002
21. *The Royal Tenenbaums* screenplay (introduction), Wes Anderson and Owen Wilson, Faber & Faber, 2001
22. *The Royal Tenenbaums* press kit, Touchstone Pictures, 2001
23. *The Wes Anderson Collection*, Matt Zoller Seitz, Abrams, 2013
24. Ibid.
25. *The Wes Anderson Collection*, Matt Zoller Seitz, Abrams, 2013
26. *The Royal Tenenbaums* screenplay, Wes Anderson and Owen Wilson, Faber & Faber, 2001
27. *The Royal Tenenbaums* international press conference, 3 September 2002
28. *The Royal Tenenbaums* press kit, Touchstone Pictures, 2001
29. Ibid.
30. *Film Threat*, Tim Merrill, 6 December 2001
31. *Entertainment Weekly*, Lisa Schwartzbaum, 22 December 2001
32. *The Royal Tenenbaums* screenplay, Wes Anderson and Owen Wilson, Faber & Faber, 2001
33. *The Royal Tenenbaums* press kit, Touchstone Pictures, 2001

THE LIFE AQUATIC WITH STEVE ZISSOU

1. *The Royal Tenenbaums* international press conference, 3 September 2002
2. *The Wes Anderson Collection*, Matt Zoller Seitz, Abrams, 2013
3. *BBC.com*, Stella Papamichael, 28 October 2004
4. *The Life Aquatic with Steve Zissou* press kit, Touchstone Pictures, 2005
5. Ibid.
6. Ibid.
7. *BBC.com*, Stella Papamichael, 28 October 2004
8. *The Wes Anderson Collection*, Matt Zoller Seitz, Abrams, 2013
9. *The Life Aquatic with Steve Zissou* press kit, Touchstone Pictures, 2005
10. Ibid.
11. *New York Magazine*, Ken Tucker, 20 December 2004
12. *The Life Aquatic with Steve Zissou* screenplay, Wes Anderson and Noah Baumbach, Touchstone Pictures, 2004
13. *The Wes Anderson Collection*, Matt Zoller Seitz, Abrams, 2013
14. *BBC.com*, Stella Papamichael, 28 October 2004
15. *The Life Aquatic with Steve Zissou* screenplay, Wes Anderson and Noah Baumbach, Touchstone Pictures, 2004
16. *The Life Aquatic with Steve Zissou* press kit, Touchstone Pictures, 2005
17. Ibid.
18. New York Film Academy, Orson Welles, 6 June 2014 (posted)
19. *The Life Aquatic with Steve Zissou* press kit, Touchstone Pictures, 2005
20. Ibid.
21. *The Wes Anderson Collection*, Matt Zoller Seitz, Abrams, 2013
22. *New York Magazine*, Ken Tucker, 20 December 2004
23. *The Wes Anderson Collection*, Matt Zoller Seitz, Abrams, 2013
24. Ibid.
25. *New York Times* live Q&A, David Carr, February 2014
26. *The New Yorker*, Richard Brody, 26 October 2009
27. *New York Magazine*, Ken Tucker, 20 December 2004
28. *The Independent*, Anthony Quinn, 18 February 2005
29. *The New Yorker*, Anthony Lane, 15 January 2005
30. *Esquire*, Ryan Reed, 24 December 2014
31. *The Life Aquatic with Steve Zissou* screenplay, Wes Anderson and Noah Baumbach, Touchstone Pictures, 2004
32. *New York Magazine*, Ken Tucker, 20 December 2004
33. *The Cinema of Ozu Yasujiro: Histories of the Everyday*, Edinburgh University Press, 2017

THE DARJEELING LIMITED

1. *The Wes Anderson Collection*, Matt Zoller Seitz, Abrams, 2013
2. *Huffington Post*, Karin Brady, 26 September 2007
3. *The Darjeeling Limited* press kit, Fox Searchlight Pictures, 2007
4. *Collider*, Steve 'Frosty' Weintraub, 7 October 2007
5. Ibid.
6. *The Wes Anderson Collection*, Matt Zoller Seitz, Abrams, 2013
7. *Collider*, Steve 'Frosty' Weintraub, 7 October 2007
8. *Screen Anarchy*, Michael Guillen, 10 October 2007
9. *The Darjeeling Limited* press kit, Fox Searchlight Pictures, 2007
10. *IndieLondon*, unattributed, October 2007
11. *Screen Anarchy*, Michael Guillen, 10 October 2007
12. *Collider*, Steve 'Frosty' Weintraub, 7 October 2007
13. *The Wes Anderson Collection*, Matt Zoller Seitz, Abrams, 2013
14. *Huffington Post*, Karin Brady, 26 September 2007
15. Ibid.
16. *The Darjeeling Limited* press kit, Fox Searchlight Pictures, 2007
17. Ibid.
18. Ibid.
19. Ibid.
20. *The New Yorker*, Richard Brody, 27 September 2009
21. *Entertainment Weekly*, Lisa Schwartzbaum, 26 September 2007
22. *The Wes Anderson Collection*, Matt Zoller Seitz, Abrams, 2013
23. Ibid.
24. *The Darjeeling Limited* DVD, Twentieth Century Fox, 2007
25. *Screen Anarchy*, Michael Guillen, 10 October 2007
26. *IndieLondon*, unattributed, October 2007
27. Ibid.
28. *Screen Anarchy*, Michael Guillen, 10 October 2007

FANTASTIC MR. FOX

1. *The Wes Anderson Collection*, Matt Zoller Seitz, Abrams, 2013
2. *The Telegraph*, Craig McLean, 20 October 2009
3. *DP/30* television interview, unattributed, 15 April 2012 (posted)
4. *The Wes Anderson Collection*, Matt Zoller Seitz, Abrams, 2013
5. Ibid.
6. Ibid.
7. *DP/30* television interview, unattributed, 15 April 2012 (posted)
8. Ibid.
9. Ibid.
10. *Fantastic Mr. Fox* Blu-ray, Criterion Collection, 28 February 2014
11. *The New Yorker*, Richard Brody, 26 October 2009
12. *DP/30* television interview, unattributed, 15 April 2012 (posted)
13. *Time Out London*, Dave Calhoun, October 2009
14. *DP/30* television interview, unattributed, 15 April 2012 (posted)
15. Ibid.
16. *Fantastic Mr. Fox* Blu-ray (behind the scenes footage), Criterion Collection, 28 February 2014
17. *The New Yorker*, Richard Brody, 26 October 2009
18. *Los Angeles Times*, Chris Lee, 11 October 2009

19. *DP/30* television interview, unattributed, 15 April 2012 (posted)
20. *Interview*, Arnaud Desplechin, 26 October 2009
21. *The New Yorker*, Richard Brody, 26 October 2009
22. Ibid.
23. *DP/30* television interview, unattributed, 15 April 2012 (posted)
24. *The New Republic*, Christopher Orr, 26 November 2009
25. *DP/30* television interview, unattributed, 15 April 2012 (posted)

MOONRISE KINGDOM

1. *Fresh Air Interview*, Terri Gross, 30 May 2012
2. *Entertainment Weekly*, Rob Brunner, 10 April 2012
3. Ibid.
4. *CNN*, Mike Ayers, 24 May 2012
5. *The New Yorker*, Anthony Lane, 28 May 2012
6. *NPR*, unattributed, 29 May 2012
7. *Fast Company*, Ari Karpel, 27 April 2012
8. *Heyuguys*, Craig Skinner, 18 May 2012
9. *The Guardian*, Francesca Babb, 19 May 2012
10. *Fast Company*, Ari Karpel, 27 April 2012
11. Ibid.
12. *CNN*, Mike Ayers, 24 May 2012
13. *Hollywood Reporter*, Gregg Kilday, 15 May 2012
14. *The Wes Anderson Collection*, Matt Zoller Seitz, Abrams, 2013
15. *Moonrise Kingdom* screenplay, Wes Anderson and Roman Coppola, Faber & Faber, 25 May 2012
16. Ibid.
17. *NPR*, unattributed, 29 May 2012
18. *Esquire*, Scott Rabb, 23 May 2012
19. *Hollywood Reporter*, Gregg Kilday, 15 May 2012
20. *Moonrise Kingdom* screenplay, Wes Anderson and Roman Coppola, Faber & Faber, 25 May 2012
21. *NPR*, unattributed, 29 May 2012
22. *Entertainment Weekly*, Rob Brunner, 10 April 2012
23. *Esquire*, Scott Rabb, 23 May 2012
24. *The Wes Anderson Collection*, Matt Zoller Seitz, Abrams, 2013
25. *The Atlantic*, Christopher Orr, 1 June 2012
26. *The Life Aquatic with Steve Zissou* press kit, Touchstone Pictures, 2005
27. *The Wes Anderson Collection*, Matt Zoller Seitz, Abrams, 2013
28. *The Observer*, Philip French, 27 May 2012
29. *Hollywood Reporter*, Gregg Kilday, 15 May 2012
30. *The New Republic*, David Thomson, 4 June 2012

THE GRAND BUDAPEST HOTEL

1. *The Guardian*, Suzie Mackenzie, 12 February 2005
2. *Esquire*, Ryan Reed, 24 December 2014
3. *YouTube*, 28 December 2012
4. *YouTube*, 18 April 2019 (posted)
5. *Time Out London*, Dave Calhoun, 4 March 2014

6. *The Telegraph*, Robbie Collin, 19 February 2014
7. *The Grand Budapest Hotel*, Matt Zoller Seitz, Abrams, 2015
8. Ibid.
9. Ibid.
10. *Time Out London*, Dave Calhoun, 4 March 2014
11. *Collider*, Steve 'Frosty' Weintraub, 24 February 2014
12. *The Grand Budapest Hotel*, Matt Zoller Seitz, Abrams, 2015
13. Ibid.
14. *Collider*, Steve 'Frosty' Weintraub, 24 February 2014
15. *The Grand Budapest Hotel*, Matt Zoller Seitz, Abrams, 2015
16. Ibid.
17. *The Society of Crossed Keys* (introductory conversation), Stefan Zweig, Pushkin Press, 2014
18. *The Telegraph*, Robbie Collin, 19 February 2014
19. *Time Out London*, Dave Calhoun, 4 March 2014
20. *The Grand Budapest Hotel*, Matt Zoller Seitz, Abrams, 2015
21. Ibid.
22. Ibid.
23. *Time*, Richard Corliss, 10 March 2014
24. *Collider*, Steve 'Frosty' Weintraub, 24 February 2014
25. *Time Out London*, Dave Calhoun, 4 March 2014
26. *New Republic*, David Thomson, 6 March 2014
27. *The Grand Budapest Hotel*, Matt Zoller Seitz, Abrams, 2015
28. *Film Comment*, Jonathan Romney, 12 March 2014
29. *The Grand Budapest Hotel* screenplay, Wes Anderson, Faber & Faber, 2014
30. Ibid.

ISLE OF DOGS

1. *Entertainment Weekly*, Piya Sinha-Roy, 22 March 2018
2. *Hollywood Reporter*, Marc Bernadin, 29 March 2018
3. *The Guardian*, Steve Rose, 26 March 2018
4. Ibid.
5. *GQ*, Anna Peele, 22 March 2018
6. *Little White Lies*, Sophie Monks Kaufman, 24 March 2018
7. *The New Yorker*, Ian Crouch, 21 June 2012
8. *Time Out London*, Gail Tolley, 23 March 2018
9. Ibid.
10. Ibid.
11. *Japan Forward*, Katsuro Fujii, 9 June 2018
12. Ibid.
13. Ibid.
14. *Isle of Dogs*, Taylor Ramos and Tony Zhou, Abrams, 2018
15. *Entertainment Weekly*, Piya Sinha-Roy, 22 March 2018
16. *GQ*, Anna Peele, 22 March 2018
17. *Little White Lies*, Sophie Monks Kaufman, 24 March 2018
18. *GQ*, Anna Peele, 22 March 2018
19. *The Guardian*, Peter Bradshaw, 29 March 2018
20. *Isle of Dogs*, Taylor Ramos and Tony Zhou, Abrams, 2018
21. Ibid.
22. *Isle of Dogs* screenplay, Wes Anderson, Faber & Faber, 2018
23. *Isle of Dogs*, Taylor Ramos and Tony Zhou, Abrams, 2018
24. *Close-ups: Wes Anderson*, Sophie Monks Kaufman, William Collins, 2018
25. *Time Out London*, Gail Tolley, 23 March 2018

THE FRENCH DISPATCH

1. *Close-ups: Wes Anderson*, Sophie Monks Kaufman, William Collins, 2018
2. *Passion Passport*, Britton Perelman, 28 May 2018
3. *Time Out*, Gail Tolley, 23 March 2018
4. *The Playlist*, Kevin Jagernauth, 18 January 2010
5. Collider.com
6. *Charente Libre*, Richard Tallet, 11 April 2019
7. *Just Enough Liebling*, A.J. Liebling, North Point Press, 2004
8. *IndieWire*, Zack Sharf, 23 March 2020
9. Ibid.
10. *IndieWire*, Zack Sharf, 20 March 2020
11. Ibid.
12. Ibid.
13. Ibid.
14. *GQ*, Anna Peele, 22 March 2018
15. *Esquire*, R. Kurt Osenlund, 7 March 2014
16. Ibid.
17. *The Grand Budapest Hotel* screenplay, Wes Anderson, Faber & Faber, 2014

ACKNOWLEDGMENTS

As ever with this growing series on what I like to think of as the most significant directors of the moment, my gratitude goes first to the man himself – Wes Anderson. It has been such a pleasure to roam through his elegant, finely measured worlds, and get a sense of the depths of feeling that lie beneath their pretty surface. I have emerged a greater fan than the enthusiast who began this voyage – and I am starting to be convinced that Bill Murray may be the finest actor of his generation (send arguments for and against to the usual address). Outside of highfalutin academic circles, there are surprisingly few books published on such a rich subject as Anderson, and I hope I have gone some way to place him and his films in a cultural context. In this, I am indebted, of course, to my editor Peter Jorgensen at Quarto for his encouragement (and subtlety with a nag) and Joe Hallsworth for calm course correction, to eagle-eyed copy-editor Nick Freeth for making sense of my prose, and to Sue Pressley at Stonecastle Graphics for making me look good, and for the patience to go with her design skills. My thanks also go to all those who have offered advice and insight and borne my Steve Zissou-like delusions of grandeur along the way (there are many). And lastly my love and appreciation continue for Kat, who likes to keep things in pretty boxes.

PICTURE CREDITS

AF archive/Alamy Stock Photo 12, 14–15,18–19r, 22, 26a, 47, 61, 70, 74, 96–97r, 101b, 104, 152; Allstar Picture Library/Alamy Stock Photo 86; Backgrid/Alamy Stock Photo 143r; BFA/Alamy Stock Photo 8–9, 142–143l; Collection Christophel/Alamy Stock Photo 6, 10, 13, 20, 21, 24, 63, 65, 68b, 72, 78, 98b, 99,102, 108, 109a, 110–111r, 112, 138–139a; Entertainment Pictures/Alamy Stock Photo 16–17, 26b, 28, 29, 52, 64, 66–67, 68a, 75, 79, 106–107, 147, 153b, 163, 164l,164–165r,166, 167, 168, 169a, 169b, 170, 171; Everett Collection Inc/Alamy Stock Photo 11, 23b,30, 32, 36b, 39a, 41a, 41b, 43, 48, 76, 98a, 103, 105, 110, 121, 123a, 150, 153a,154–155l; Featureflash Archive/Alamy Stock Photo 126; dpa picture alliance/Alamy Stock Photo 133b; Geisler-Fotopress GmbH/Alamy Stock Photo 162; Gtres Información más Comuniación on line, S.L./Alamy Stock Photo 146; LANDMARK MEDIA/Alamy Stock Photo 148, 149, 151, 155b, 156, 157, 158a, 158–159b; Moviestore Collection Ltd/Alamy Stock Photo 132, 159a, 159br, 161; Nathaniel Noir/Alamy Stock Photo 71; parkerphotography/Alamy Stock Photo 100; Photo 12/Alamy Stock Photo 34, 38, 39b, 44, 46, 49, 50, 57, 58, 59, 60, 69, 96l, 101a, 109b, 123b, 130, 137b; Pictorial Press Ltd/Alamy Stock Photo 30–31r, 82, 160; PictureLux/The Hollywood Archive/Alamy Stock Photo 23a, 33, 35, 36a, 40, 62; ScreenProd/Photononstop/Alamy Stock Photo 37; Sportsphoto/Alamy Stock Photo 18, 81, 144; TCD/Prod.DB/Alamy Stock Photo 25, 27, 42, 51, 53a, 53b, 54, 55, 73, 77, 80, 83, 84–85, 87, 88a, 88b, 89, 90, 91, 92, 93, 94, 95, 112, 114, 115, 116–117, 118, 119a, 119b, 120, 122a, 122b, 124–125b, 125a, 127, 128, 129, 131,133a, 134, 135, 136, 137a, 139b, 140a, 140b, 141, 145; United Archives GmbH/Alamy Stock Photo 56; WENN Rights Ltd/Alamy Stock Photo 7.

GATEFOLD INSERT PICTURE CREDITS

Bottle Rocket poster: Everett Collection, Inc./Alamy Stock Photo; *Rushmore* poster: Everett Collection, Inc./Alamy Stock Photo; *The Royal Tenenbaums* poster: AF archive/Alamy Stock Photo; *The Life Aquatic* poster: Collection Christophel/Alamy Stock Photo; *The Squid and the Whale* poster: Photo 12/Alamy Stock Photo; Peter Bogdanovic: PictureLux/The Hollywood Archive/Alamy Stock Photo; *Hotel Chevalier*: Allstar Picture Library/Alamy Stock Photo; *The Darjeeling Limited* poster: Sportsphoto/Alamy Stock Photo; *Fantastic Mr. Fox* poster: Photo 12/Alamy Stock Photo; Roman Coppola: AF archive/Alamy Stock Photo; James Ivory: colaimages/Alamy Stock Photo; *Moonrise Kingdom* poster: TCD/Prod.DB/Alamy Stock Photo; *The Grand Budapest Hotel*: TCD/Prod.DB/Alamy Stock Photo; *She's Funny That Way* poster: Everett Collection Inc/Alamy Stock Photo; Bar Luce: Marina Spironetti/Alamy Stock Photo; *Sing* poster: Everett Collection Inc/Alamy Stock Photo; *Escapes* poster: Everett Collection Inc/Alamy Stock Photo; *Isle of Dogs* poster: Entertainment Pictures/Alamy Stock Photo; Spitzmaus Mummy in a Coffin and other Treasures Exhibition: Independent Photo Agency Srl/Alamy Stock Photo; *The French Dispatch* poster: Entertainment Pictures/Alamy Stock Photo.